NEW DIRECTIONS FOR COMMUNITY COLLEGES

Arthur M. Cohen
EDITOR-IN-CHIEF

Florence B. Brawer
ASSOCIATE EDITOR

D0916533

Creating and Maintaining a Diverse Faculty

William B. Harvey
North Carolina State University

James Valadez
North Carolina State University

EDITORS

Number 87, Fall 1994

JOSSEY-BASS PUBLISHERS
San Francisco

Clearinghouse for Community Colleges

CREATING AND MAINTAINING A DIVERSE FACULTY
William B. Harvey, James Valadez (eds.)
New Directions for Community Colleges, no. 87
Volume XXII, number 3
Arthur M. Cohen, Editor-in-Chief
Florence B. Brawer, Associate Editor

Microfilm copies of issues and articles are available in 16mm and 35mm, as well as microfiche in 105mm, through University Microfilms Inc., 300 North Zeeb Road, Ann Arbor, Michigan 48106-1346.

LC 85-644753   ISSN 0194-3081   ISBN 0-7879-9982-2

NEW DIRECTIONS FOR COMMUNITY COLLEGES is part of The Jossey-Bass Higher and Adult Education Series and is published quarterly by Jossey-Bass Inc., Publishers, 350 Sansome Street, San Francisco, California 94104-1342 (publication number USPS 121-710) in association with the ERIC Clearinghouse for Community Colleges. Second-class postage paid at San Francisco, California, and at additional mailing offices. POST-MASTER: Send address changes to New Directions for Community Colleges, Jossey-Bass Inc., Publishers, 350 Sansome Street, San Francisco, California 94104-1342.

SUBSCRIPTIONS for 1994 cost $49.00 for individuals and $72.00 for institutions, agencies, and libraries.

THE MATERIAL in this publication is based on work sponsored wholly or in part by the Office of Educational Research and Improvement, U.S. Department of Education, under contract number RI 93-00-2003. Its contents do not necessarily reflect the views of the Department, or any other agency of the U.S. Government.

EDITORIAL CORRESPONDENCE should be sent to the Editor-in-Chief, Arthur M. Cohen, at the ERIC Clearinghouse for Community Colleges, University of California, 3051 Moore Hall, 405 Hilgard Avenue, Los Angeles, California 90024-1521.

Cover photograph © Rene Sheret, After Image, Los Angeles, California, 1990.

Manufactured in the United States of America. Nearly all Jossey-Bass books, jackets, and periodicals are printed on recycled paper that contains at least 50 percent recycled waste, including 10 percent postconsumer waste. Many of our materials are also printed with vegetable-based inks; during the printing process these inks emit fewer volatile organic compounds (VOCs) than petroleum-based inks. VOCs contribute to the formation of smog.

CONTENTS

EDITORS' NOTES

One of the most vexing issues facing higher education generally, and community colleges specifically, is the underrepresentation of minority faculty members, particularly African Americans and Hispanics. The concern is both symbolic and substantive since faculty are at the heart of the academic experience.

Faculty provide knowledge, insights, guidance, direction, and inspiration, influencing students beyond the bounds of their subject matter. Their wisdom and experience make faculty role models in matters of behavior, decorum, and values (Harvey, 1991, p. 117). Because institutions are enriched by the perspectives and considerations of minority faculty members, both students and colleagues gain immeasurably from their presence.

Despite the widespread support voiced for increasing minority faculty representation, the proportion of faculty positions held by minorities has not increased substantially. Researchers have suggested reasons for this phenomenon that range from structural barriers to shortages of qualified personnel to attitudinal resistance in increased minority presence. Practitioners have identified processes, strategies, and approaches that might be used to increase the numbers of minority faculty members. Neither the best of intentions nor the best laid plans alone have resolved this dilemma, but perhaps combining them can yield greater representation of African Americans and Hispanics among the community college faculty ranks.

This volume, "Creating and Maintaining a Diverse Faculty," focuses on African Americans and Hispanics and presents both theoretical and practical considerations of scholars and administrators on the subject of minority faculty representation. In Chapter One, Deborah Carter presents a broad overview of the national situation regarding minority faculty, including findings from both two- and four-year institutions. In Chapter Two, William B. Harvey suggests an approach for getting a critical mass of African American faculty on a campus. In Chapter Three, Dorothy Knoell examines what is happening in California regarding the hiring of minority faculty. In Chapter Four, Freddie Nicholas and Arnie Oliver identify how campus leadership can enhance the hiring of minority faculty. Ronald Opp and Albert Smith present the results of a national survey on minority faculty in Chapter Five. In Chapter Six, Jerry Sue Owens, Frank Reis, and Kathryn Hall suggest that the "open door" of community colleges be used to let minority faculty in as well as students. In Chapter Seven, Piedad Robertson and Ted Frier explore the significance of minority faculty as role models. In Chapter Eight, Alfredo de los Santos presents the successes of the Maricopa Community College system in pursuing diversity. In Chapter Nine, James Valadez examines how values and attitudes influence the climate for minority faculty. Finally, Frankie Laanan offers an

1

annotated bibliography of sources of information on recruiting and maintaining minority faculty in Chapter Ten.

The higher education community, especially community colleges, must be responsive to the increasing diversity of the American citizenry. This volume is intended to facilitate both the discussion and the action necessary to achieve a more racially and ethnically representative faculty in two-year colleges.

> William B. Harvey
> James Valadez
> Editors

Reference

Harvey, W. B. "Faculty Responsibility and Racial Tolerance." *Thought and Action: The NEA Higher Education Journal,* 1991, 7 (2), 115–136.

WILLIAM B. HARVEY is professor of higher education, adult and community college education, North Carolina State University, Raleigh.

JAMES VALADEZ is assistant professor of adult and community college education, North Carolina State University, Raleigh.

A challenge for community college leaders will be to move beyond the rhetoric and push for increasing the employment opportunities for faculty of color.

The Status of Faculty in Community Colleges: What Do We Know?

Deborah J. Carter

Internal and external pressures on higher education have intensified to such a level that many more university leaders are questioning how to reshape their institutions to be more responsive to major societal shifts that engulf our nation and world. Forces that are pressuring changes on our campuses include expanding knowledge and technology, changing racial and ethnic demographics juxtaposed with inadequate educational and employment opportunities for persons of color, and increasing internationalism. Among the greatest challenges for America in the 1990s and beyond will be educating and employing its increasingly diverse population in a shrinking and rapidly changing global society. To use the words of leading demographer William O'Hare, "The United States is undergoing a transition from a predominantly white population rooted in Western culture to a society composed of people from diverse racial and ethnic backgrounds" (1992, p. 2).

How well and how quickly colleges and universities improve their response to the challenge of educating students of color depends, in large part, on how well and how quickly they can create a higher education faculty and leadership infrastructure capable of dealing with both the opportunities and the challenges inherent in a truly diverse student population. To be successful, predominantly white institutions must include a sufficient number of faculty and administrators of color who have sufficient influence and authority to have an impact on the courses these institutions take. Although most colleges and universities espouse the goal of increasing the number of minority faculty on campus, employment growth among faculty of color has been uneven at best, and overall minority representation remains relatively small on most predominantly white campuses.

NEW DIRECTIONS FOR COMMUNITY COLLEGES, no. 87, Fall 1994 © Jossey-Bass Publishers

3

During the 1980s and early 1990s, as colleges and universities increased faculty to meet growing student enrollment needs, the collective share of full-time positions held by African American, Hispanic, and American Indian faculty only increased from 6 percent in 1981 to 7 percent by 1991 (Equal Employment Opportunity Commission surveys, 1981 and 1991). Despite numerical gains made by these groups, underrepresentation of African American, Hispanic, and American Indian faculty remains evident on the vast majority of college and university campuses. The overall representation of minority faculty on both two- and four-year campuses is considerably lower than the ratio of students of color. Given the high concentration of students of color in community colleges, one might expect these institutions to employ a larger proportion of faculty of color than four-year campuses do. This is not the case. Overall, faculty of color hold approximately the same percentage of full-time appointments in two-year institutions as they do in four-year colleges and universities, while students of color comprise a larger percentage of two-year student bodies than four-year student populations—24.4 percent compared to 18.1 percent (U.S. Department of Education, 1993).

Although data on faculty of color in two-year colleges are limited, this chapter offers a brief profile of full-time and part-time African American, Hispanic, American Indian, and Asian American faculty in this sector. Since the Equal Employment Opportunity Commission's EEO-6 survey only disaggregates data for public and private institutions, and not by institutional type, little national data are available on long-term racial/ethnic employment trends in two-year and four-year colleges and universities. This scarcity of data presents a continuing dilemma to researchers and policy makers, which must be addressed by federal agencies responsible for monitoring hiring and employment practices in higher education.

The 1989–1990 survey of faculty conducted by Higher Education Research Institute (HERI) at University of California, Los Angeles, and the 1987 National Survey of Postsecondary Faculty (NSOPF-88) by the National Center for Education Statistics (NCES) are two of the few sources of employment data on faculty of color in two-year colleges. Data from these studies are used extensively throughout this chapter. Descriptive data are presented on the distribution of minority faculty by gender, academic rank, tenure status, discipline, highest degree earned, and salary level for full-time faculty of color, and where available, the same data are analyzed for part-time faculty of color. Data contained in this profile clearly suggest that concentrated and sustained recruitment and retention efforts continue to be critical to expand the number of faculty of color within the two-year college sector.

Employment of Full-Time Faculty of Color

The continued underrepresentation of African American, American Indian, and Hispanic faculty is evidenced in both two-year and four-year institutions. Although Asian American faculty are not proportionally underrepresented in

Table 1.1. Racial and Ethnic Distribution of Faculty
by Institutional Type, 1989–1990 (Percentages)

	All		Two-Year Colleges		Four-Year Colleges		Universities	
	Two-Year	Four-Year	Public	Private	Public	Private	Public	Private
White	91.2	90.2	90.0	97.4	86.8	91.7	91.6	93.3
Total faculty of color	9.3	9.1	9.6	2.6	12.6	8.1	7.7	5.5
African American	4.0	3.9	4.1	2.6	7.0	4.0	1.4	2.0
American Indian	1.2	0.8	1.3	0.0	1.0	0.6	0.9	0.4
Asian American	2.2	3.4	2.3	0.0	3.8	2.1	4.2	2.8
Mexican American	1.7	0.5	1.7	0.0	0.6	0.3	0.8	0.2
Puerto Rican American	0.2	0.5	0.2	0.0	0.2	1.1	0.4	0.1
Other	1.7	2.2	1.8	0.0	2.2	1.8	2.6	2.3

Note: Percentages may not add to 100 due to rounding.

Source: Astin, Korn, and Dey, 1991. Reproduced by permission of the authors.

the four-year sector, they remain scarce in certain fields and on two-year campuses. They face many of the same barriers and circumstances that other ethnic
minority faculty encounter throughout higher education. According to national
data, faculty of color hold nearly equal shares of full-time faculty appointments
in two-year and four-year institutions—9.3 percent and 9.1 percent respectively (Table 1.1). Percentages are higher in public institutions, with faculty of
color holding 9.6 percent of all full-time faculty appointments in public two-
year colleges and 12.6 percent at public four-year colleges. Private institutions
show lower percentages—8.1 percent at private four-year colleges, 7.7 percent
at private universities, and 2.6 percent at private two-year colleges. The NCES's
1987 faculty survey revealed a slightly larger difference—11 percent of full-
time faculty in four-year institutions are minorities compared to 9 percent in
two-year public colleges.

It is important to note, however, that 30 percent of all full-time African
American faculty are employed in approximately 55 public four-year historically black colleges and universities (HBCU's). This estimate is derived from
the 1989–90 HERI faculty survey, the United Negro College Fund faculty survey, and the 1975–1989 EEO-6 survey. Consequently, the number of African
Americans employed in public four-year HBCU's greatly increases the overall
representation of faculty of color in this sector. Figures reported in this chapter
include HBCU's, tribal colleges, and Hispanic-serving institutions (HSIs)—two-
year and four-year campuses with 25 percent or more Hispanic American student enrollment. Similarly, using data from the NSOPF-88 and The American

Indian Higher Education Consortium faculty survey, estimates show one-quarter of all American Indian faculty on two-year campuses are employed by 22 two-year tribal colleges (O'Brien, 1992). African American, American Indian, and Hispanic faculty are concentrated in these types of institutions. National data are not currently available to compare the representation of faculty of color in two-year and four-year predominantly white institutions (PWIs). It is estimated that faculties at PWIs are only about 2 percent African American (Carter and Wilson, 1992).

The exact percentage of Asian American, African American, Hispanic American, and American Indian faculty in two-year colleges varies by one to two percentage points, depending on the data source (see Table 1.2). The percentages of minority two-year faculty in the HERI 1989–90 and NSOPF-88 studies—both faculty sample surveys—are in closer agreement than data from Opp and Smith (1992), which provides the most recent national data for faculty of color on two-year campuses. Opp and Smith collected and analyzed institutional self-reported data, which yielded racial and ethnic counts slightly higher than weighted data gathered from the HERI and NCES faculty sample surveys. Opp and Smith provide several plausible reasons for this variation, including the possibility that minority faculty may have had lower response rates on these sample surveys that affected the weighting procedures used to estimate the total faculty population. Also, institutions reporting faculty data in the institutional self-study may not have been representative of the total two-year college population; those responding may have employed higher percentages of faculty of color than those that did not respond. Despite variations in these three studies, they do provide some indications about racial/ethnic distribution of minority faculty in this sector.

According to the HERI study, African Americans hold 4 percent of all full-time faculty appointments in two-year public colleges, followed by Asian Americans with 2.2 percent, Hispanic American (those identified as Mexican American, Chicano, or Puerto Rican) with 1.9 percent, and American Indians

Table 1.2. Percentage of Faculty of Color in Two-Year Institutions

	Opp and Smith 1991–92	HERI 1989–90	NSOPF-88
African American	5.1%	4.0%	3%
American Indian	1.4	1.2	1
Asian American	—	2.2	2
Latino/Latina	—	—	3
Mexican American	1.7	1.7	—
Puerto Rican American	0.3	0.2	—
Total	8.5	9.3	9

Note: The Opp and Smith 1991–92 survey did not analyze the representation of Asian American faculty; total excludes Asian American faculty.

Sources: Astin, Korn, and Dey, 1991; Opp and Smith, 1992; National Center for Education Statistics, 1990.

with 1.2 percent. The findings from the Opp and Smith study show the largest percentage of African American faculty—5.1 percent. In comparison, the NSOPF-88 data indicate the lowest percentage of African American faculty at 3 percent, equivalent to the percentage of Hispanic faculty. The percentage of American Indian faculty is fairly consistent in all three studies, ranging from 1 to 1.4 percent. Asian Americans hold approximately 2 percent of two-year faculty positions, a lower representation than in four-year colleges and universities (see Table 1.3).

**Table 1.3. Annual Hiring Patterns of Faculty of Color
and Full-Time Faculty by Institutional Type,
1987–88 to 1992–93**

	Percentage of Institutions with Net Gains or Net Losses				
	Total	Two-Year	Baccalaureate	Comprehensive	Doctoral
Change in Faculty of Color					
1987–88 to 1988–89:					
Net Gain	24%	21%	14%	37%	60%
Net Loss	6	4	7	11	6
1988–89 to 1989–90:					
Net Gain	41	39	32	51	63
Net Loss	7	6	8	10	3
1989–90 to 1990–91:					
Net Gain	37	34	28	46	69
Net Loss	7	7	5	12	2
1990–91 to 1991–92:					
Net Gain	34	29	33	38	50
Net Loss	6	6	0	9	11
1991–92 to 1992–93:					
Net Gain	40	42	23	44	57
Net Loss	8	7	7	10	9
Change in Full-Time Faculty					
1987–88 to 1988–89:					
Net Gain	52	47	51	64	65
Net Loss	8	8	6	12	10
1988–89 to 1989–90:					
Net Gain	63	63	59	69	66
Net Loss	9	9	8	11	16
1989–90 to 1990–91:					
Net Gain	58	64	56	50	52
Net Loss	11	11	3	24	18
1990–91 to 1991–92:					
Net Gain	48	44	45	57	49
Net Loss	20	20	14	22	31
1991–92 to 1992–93:					
Net Gain	49	46	57	52	40
Net Loss	22	23	7	28	35

Source: El-Khawas, 1989–1993. Reproduced by permission of the author.

Because EEO-6 survey data are not currently disaggregated by institutional types, annual trend data on the number of faculty of color employed on two-year campuses are unavailable. However, the *Campus Trends* surveys, conducted annually by El-Khawas since 1984, do offer some indication of net gains and losses in percentage of minority faculty employed at two-year institutions. *Campus Trends* data show that the annual percentages of institutions reporting changes in the number of faculty employed vary by institutional type. This finding holds true for faculty of color as well. The percentage of colleges and universities reporting changes in the number of minority faculty employed on campus for the five-year period between 1988–89 and 1992–93 is shown in Table 1.3.

Several noteworthy trends are evidenced in the *Campus Trends* data. First, more two-year colleges, baccalaureate, and comprehensive institutions reported net gains in total full-time faculty than reported gains in the number of minority faculty employed. However, these differences may reflect a number of factors including the concentration of faculty of color on relatively few campuses and a possible slower growth rate for minority faculty than for total faculty within these sectors. By contrast, the percentage of doctoral universities reporting overall faculty employment gains and increases in minority faculty was fairly equal during this five-year period.

However, given the larger representation of Asian American than other faculty of color in doctoral institutions, as well as a rapid overall growth rate of Asian Americans, it can be assumed that Asian American faculty account for much of the minority faculty employment growth reported by institutions in this sector. According to EEO-6 survey data, between 1981 and 1991 the number of Asian American faculty employed in higher education grew at the fastest rate compared to other racial and ethnic groups. During this period, Asian American faculty increased by 78 percent, while Hispanic faculty experienced a 58 percent gain and African American and American Indian faculty netted 25 percent and 16 percent increases, respectively. However, EEOC data also reveal that a large percentage of Asian faculty—approximately 40 percent—are non–U.S. citizens (Carter and Wilson, 1992). This means that about 3 percent of all higher education faculty are U.S.–born or naturalized Asian Americans. Other ethnic minority faculty continue to be grossly underrepresented in public and private universities (Table 1.1).

Second, *Campus Trends* (El-Kahwas, 1989, 1990, 1991, 1992, and 1993) surveys reveal that relatively few colleges and universities reported losses in the overall number of faculty of color employed, while a growing number reported losses in full-time faculty positions. During this five-year period, the number of colleges and universities reporting net losses in faculty increased from 8 to 22 percent, while the number reporting losses in faculty of color held fairly steady, ranging between 6 and 8 percent. The same trend was evident at two-year campuses—the number of two-year campuses reporting losses in full-time faculty increased from 8 percent between 1987–88 and 1988–89 to 23 percent between 1991–92 and 1992–93, while the number of two-year institutions reporting losses in the number of faculty of color increased only 3 percentage points (4 percent to 7 percent) during this same period (Table 1.3). These data tend to indicate that, although nearly one-quarter of all two-year and four-year institutions are in the process of downsizing their faculty, most are not losing ground in the number of minority faculty.

Tenure and Academic Rank of Full-Time Faculty

Although many two-year colleges have faculty employment policies resembling the traditional tenure system, the tenure process in most two-year institutions functions differently than in four-year institutions. First, it is important to note that 25 percent of all two-year public full-time faculty are employed by institutions that do not have a tenure system (NSOPF, 1990). Second, in those community colleges that do grant tenure, it is often awarded in a shorter period of time than the seven-year standard common in universities (Cohen and Brawer, 1989). Of all two-year faculty, 70.6 percent are tenured compared to 65.7 percent of all four-year faculty (Astin, Korn, and Dey, 1991). Although national data on the tenure rates for faculty of color in two-year colleges is extremely limited, it appears that minority faculty are also tenured at somewhat higher rates in two-year colleges than are their counterparts on four-year campuses.

In two-year institutions, African American, American Indian, and Asian American full-time faculty hold tenured faculty positions at rates slightly above the national average for two-year faculty (Table 1.4). This may be due in large part to the lower tenure rate among white women, who hold tenured faculty positions at the lowest rate of all groups in the two-year sector—only 62 percent of white female faculty are tenured. Of African American faculty, 73.7 percent are tenured, compared to 72.5 percent of Asian American and American Indian faculty, figures just above the 70.6 percent national average for two-year faculty. According to the HERI faculty survey, Mexican American two-year faculty have the highest tenure rates—85.5 percentage.

Table 1.4. Percentage of Two-Year Faculty Holding Tenured Positions by Gender and Race/Ethnicity, 1989–90

	All	Men	Women
Total two-year faculty	70.6%	75.4%	63.2%
White	70.3	75.6	62.0
African American	73.7	71.4	75.1
American Indian	72.5	74.8	65.0
Asian American	72.5	72.5	72.4
Mexican American	85.5	85.8	85.2

Note: The tenure rates for Puerto Rican American two-year faculty are not shown because the sample size is too small to produce reliable estimates.

Source: Higher Education Research Institute, 1992. Reproduced by permission of the author.

Table 1.5. Percentage Distribution of Full-Time Two-Year Faculty
by Rank and Race/Ethnicity, 1989–90

	Full Professor	Associate Professor	Assistant Professor	Instructors/ Lecturers	Other
Total	25.1%	16.0%	12.4%	41.2%	5.3%
White	26.0	16.4	12.4	39.9	5.3
African American	14.9	14.8	13.6	51.7	5.0
American Indian	29.0	9.4	7.1	52.5	2.0
Asian American	17.2	13.8	10.0	52.8	6.2
Mexican American	20.2	10.0	7.5	56.2	6.2
Puerto Rican American	—	—	50.7	49.3	—

Source: Higher Education Research Institute, 1992. Reprinted by permission of the author.

Considerable differences exist between the tenure rates of white men and white women on two-year campuses; 75.6 percent of white men are tenured compared to 62 percent of white women. With the exception of American Indian men and women, the tenure rates of women of color approximates that of their male counterparts (Table 1.4). Additionally the percentage of Mexican American, African American, and Asian American women holding tenured faculty positions is considerably higher than that of white and American Indian women faculty.

Despite the relatively high tenure rate of two-year faculty of color, most do not fare as well as white faculty in terms of academic rank. When analyzing two-year faculty by rank, it is important to note that nearly one-third of all two-year colleges do not designate faculty by academic rank (NSOPF, 1990). However, faculty of color in two-year institutions where faculty are ranked show statistics similar to four-year institutions. American Indian, Hispanic American, African American, and Asian American faculty are more concentrated in lecturer and instructor positions than are their white counterparts. Of all full-time faculty in two-year colleges, one quarter are full professors, 16 percent are associate professors, 12.4 percent are assistant professors, and 41.2 percent are lecturers or instructors (Table 1.5). However, among faculty of color over half are either instructors or lecturers. For African Americans, 51.7 percent are lecturers or instructors. By contrast, of African American faculty, only 14.9 percent are full professors, 14.8 percent associate professors, and 13.6 percent assistant professors. Similarly, few Hispanic Americans, American Indians, and Asian Americans occupy senior faculty positions. Only 20.2 percent of Mexican Americans are full professors compared to 56.2 percent who are instructors or lecturers. Of Puerto Rican faculty on two-year campuses, half are assistant professors and the other half are instructors or lecturers. Few American Indian two-year faculty are associate or assistant professors, but, when compared to other ethnic minorities, a slightly larger percentage (29 percent) serve as full professors. However, a sizeable share of the senior faculty positions that American Indians hold may be at two-year tribal colleges. And despite Asian Americans' increasing presence among two-year faculty, they are less likely to be among the senior faculty ranks in two-year colleges. Only 17.2 percent of Asian American faculty are full professors, while 13.8 percent hold associate professor positions, 10 percent are assistant professors, and 52.8 percent are instructors or lecturers.

Educational Attainment of Faculty

Most two-year institutions do not require faculty to have a doctorate; in contrast, this functions as the required "faculty union card" on virtually all four-year campuses. Both the NSOPF-88 and the HERI 1989–90 surveys show that the educational backgrounds of two-year faculty differ from those of four-year college and university faculty. Most community college faculty (approximately 60 percent) hold a master's degree as their highest degree. Overall, approximately 30 percent of all higher education faculty (two-year and four-year combined) hold a master's degree as their highest degree. The majority of four-year faculty (61 percent) hold a Ph.D. or Ed.D., compared to about one-sixth of two-year faculty (Astin, Korn, and Dey, 1991). Additionally, 10 percent of all two-year faculty have a bachelor's as their highest degree.

Like white faculty, the largest share of two-year faculty of color hold a master's as their highest degree. While 61.4 percent of white two-year faculty hold a master's degree, 56.9 percent of African Americans, 56.7 percent of Asian Americans, 54.4 percent of Mexican Americans, 51.8 percent of American Indians, and 49.6 percent of Puerto Ricans in this sector have a master's as their highest degree (Table 1.6). Although a larger share of Asian American

Table 1.6. Highest Degree Held by All Faculty
and by Two-Year Faculty, 1989–90 (Percentages)

	All Institutions			Two-Year Institutions		
	Bachelor's	Master's	Doctorate	Bachelor's	Master's	Doctorate
Total	3.2%	28.1%	61.0%	9.8%	60.8%	16.4%
White	3.2	28.2	61.3	9.9	61.4	16.0
African American	2.9	37.4	49.1	8.7	56.9	16.2
American Indian[a]	—	—	—	9.8	51.8	18.0
Asian American	2.4	15.8	76.5	9.8	56.7	25.7
Hispanic	6.7	38.5	43.4	—	—	—
Mexican American[a]	—	—	—	11.3	54.4	14.9
Puerto Rican[a]	—	—	—	36.4	49.6	6.4

Note: Detail does not add to 100 percent because some faculty have other types of degrees that qualify them to teach.

[a] Data on the highest degrees held by American Indians at all institutions were not included in this analysis. Additionally, separate analyses of the highest degree held by Mexican American and Puerto Rican faculty were not conducted on all the institutions' data.

Source: Higher Education Research Institute, 1992. Reprinted by permission of the author.

faculty have doctoral degrees than other two-year faculty—25.7 percent compared to 16 percent of all two-year faculty—there is no significant difference between the educational attainment levels of two-year faculty based on their racial or ethnic backgrounds (HERI 1989–90, 1992).

Salary Distribution of Full-Time Faculty

In 1989–90, the median salary range for full-time two-year faculty was $40,000–$49,000 (Astin, Korn, and Dey, 1991). In general, the median salary distribution of two-year faculty of color is very close to the national median for this sector (Table 1.7). There are, however, several notable exceptions to this trend.

The first exception is the disproportionately larger share of African American and American Indian faculty earning $30,000 or less—11.2 percent of African American two-year faculty and 12.6 percent of American Indian faculty are in this salary range compared to 8.7 percent of all faculty. The reverse holds true for Mexican Americans and Asian Americans—smaller than average shares of Mexican American and Asian American two-year faculty have incomes of $30,000 or less—2.5 percent and 3.8 percent respectively. When compared to other racial and ethnic groups, a larger share of Mexican American faculty earn $60,000 or more. On average, only 21.2 percent of all two-year faculty are in this income category (31.5 percent compared to an overall 21.2 percent). It should also be noted that 1989–90 HERI data found no African American faculty earning over $70,000 among the 4.4 percent of all two-year faculty who earn these higher salaries.

Full-Time Faculty by Discipline

The top academic employment fields for faculty of color in two-year colleges only somewhat resembles the pattern in four-year institutions. The largest

Table 1.7. Salary Distribution of Full-Time, Two-Year Faculty by Race/Ethnicity, 1989–90 (Percentages)

	Below $30,000	$30,000–39,000	$40,000–49,000	$50,000–59,000	$60,000–69,000	$70,000 and Above
All faculty	8.7	17.9	31.8	20.4	16.8	4.4
White	8.9	17.5	31.7	20.7	16.7	4.6
Faculty of color	7.5	22.4	29.2	19.5	17.5	3.9
African American	11.2	26.4	22.1	20.6	19.7	—
American Indian	12.6	13.9	36.3	18.4	12.0	6.8
Asian American	3.8	25.8	32.0	23.1	11.0	4.3
Mexican American	2.5	23.6	26.4	16.0	27.1	4.4

Source: Higher Education Research Institute, 1992. Reprinted by permission of the author.

share of African American faculty in two-year colleges is employed in the social sciences (18.7 percent), followed by health-related (15.6 percent), and education departments (13 percent). Business departments rank fourth, employing 10.3 percent of the African American faculty in the two-year sector. English departments employ the largest percentage of Hispanic American Faculty (approximately 23 percent), with health-related departments (18.4 percent) ranking second, followed by the social science departments (10.2 percent), and mathematics and statistics departments (10 percent). For Asian American faculty, the top five employment fields in two-year colleges are the social sciences (15.9 percent), mathematics and statistics (14.5 percent), other technical departments (10.8 percent), business (9.7 percent), and education (9.4 percent). In four-year colleges and universities, the largest share of Asian American faculty teach in engineering, followed by the social sciences, the physical sciences, and mathematics or statistics.

Less information is available on the exact employment fields of American Indian two-year faculty. Data from the HERI faculty survey show that the two largest shares of American Indian faculty are employed in departments that are grouped as "other" or as "other technical"—21.6 percent and 14.6 percent, respectively. Based on HERI survey analyses, "other" areas include the following departments: ethnic and women studies, architecture or urban planning, home economics, law and law enforcement, library science, as well as other (Astin, Korn, and Dey, 1991). "Other technical" fields include building trades, data processing and computer sciences, drafting and design, electronics, industrial arts, and mechanics. Two other identifiably large shares of American Indian faculty are in English (10.7 percent) and the social sciences (8.2 percent).

Part-Time Minority Faculty

The use of part-time faculty is edging upward on all college campuses due to the widespread financial difficulties at many institutions (El-Khawas, 1993). Public two-year colleges continue to be the most likely to make extensive use of part-time faculty, and this trend appears to be on the rise. Part-time faculty comprise 52.1 percent of all faculty in community colleges and 34.1 percent in private two-year colleges (NSOPF-88).

National data on part-time faculty of color in community colleges are extremely limited. The NSOPF-88 is one of the few sources. Surprisingly, this study shows that community colleges employ a smaller percentage of part-time faculty of color than four-year campuses. Faculty of color hold 8 to 9 percent of part-time faculty positions in two-year colleges compared with 13 percent at four-year institutions. African Americans make up 3 percent of part-time faculty in community colleges, followed by Hispanics and Asian Americans—which each hold 2 percent. As is the case with full-time positions, American Indians represent about 1 percent of all part-time, two-year faculty positions (Table 1.8).

**Table 1.8. Percentage Distribution of Part-Time Faculty,
Fall 1987**

	All Institutions	Two-Year Public Institutions	Four-Year Institutions
Gender			
Male	56%	58%	54%
Female	44	42	46
Race/Ethnicity			
White	90	91	87
African American	4	3	4
Asian	3	2	5
Hispanic	2	2	2
American Indian	1	1	2

Note: Percentages may not add to 100 due to rounding.
Source: National Center for Education Statistics, 1990.

Male faculty hold a slightly larger share of part-time appointments than female faculty in both two-year and four-year institutions. Women represent 42 percent of part-time faculty in two-year institutions, compared to 46 percent in four-year colleges and universities (Table 1.8).

Long-term trend data are not available for part-time faculty of color in the two-year sector. However, based on general increases in the use of part-time faculty in two-year colleges, one might expect that the percentage of part-time minority faculty is also increasing. According to the *Campus Trends* survey for 1988–89, 58 percent of two-year colleges stated that they made extensive use of part-time faculty, meaning that one-fourth or more of their courses were taught by part-time instructors. By 1992–93, that percentage had increased to 73 percent of two-year colleges.

In their study, Opp and Smith (1992) found that 92 percent of the community colleges considered to have a "high" percentage of underrepresented faculty of color (5 percent or more) invited minority professionals from business and industry to serve as part-time adjunct faculty, compared to 75 percent of the institutions where less than 5 percent of the faculty were minorities. Opp and Smith suggest that employing part-time faculty of color may be one of a number of short-term strategies to increase minority faculty counts. Yet, utilizing part-time faculty does little to address the systemic issues that serve as obstacles to expanding the cadre of full-time faculty of color on two-year campuses. Therefore, the strategy of hiring part-time faculty of color should be used in tandem with other strategies to expand the number of full-time faculty of color.

Summary and Recommendations

This analysis of community college faculty provides only a snapshot of the representation and general characteristics of faculty of color. Because of the lack of national trend data, it is difficult to determine what changes have occurred over time in the number and status of faculty of color by sector. However, available data clearly indicate that while people of color represent a rapidly growing segment of the U.S population and of the college student population, they continue to be greatly and nearly equally underrepresented among faculty at both two-year and four-year campuses. Consequently, neither the two- nor the four-year sector can claim to be doing much better than the other in recruiting and retaining faculty of color. Although public two-year colleges are the most likely to make extensive use of part-time faculty, a trend that appears to be on the rise, community colleges employ a slightly smaller percentage of part-time faculty of color than do four-year campuses.

Overall, the employment status of two-year faculty of color only partially mirrors that of their four-year counterparts. Unlike four-year college and university campuses, where faculty of color hold tenure at lower than average rates, in two-year colleges African American, American Indian, Hispanic American, and Asian American full-time faculty hold tenured positions at rates slightly above the national average. However, despite the higher tenure rate of two-year faculty of color, most do not fare as well as white faculty in terms of academic rank; a much larger share of minority than white faculty are lecturers and instructors. These contrary trends in the rank and tenure of two-year faculty of color may be partially attributed to differences in the tenure and promotion system in two-year and four-year institutions.

National trend data on faculty of color in two-year colleges are extremely limited; therefore, it is nearly impossible to gauge their progress or the lack thereof. Although we do not know exactly how representation of minority faculty on two-year campuses has changed over time, we do know that during the most recent five-year period a larger number of two-year colleges experienced overall gains in the number of faculty they employ than those that netted gains in the number of minority faculty on campus. This may mean that the growth rate of minority faculty in two-year institutions is not keeping pace with the overall rate of faculty growth in this sector.

The Equal Employment Opportunity Commission and other federal agencies need to improve their data collection, analysis, and reporting mechanisms so that employment information issues may be more fully examined. EEOC provides the only ongoing national survey that includes racial and ethnic information on higher education employees; however, without the capacity to disaggregate and conduct separate analysis of EEOC survey results for two-year faculty, staff, and administrators, we are left knowing little other than that minority faculty are underrepresented in most fields and are concentrated in the lower faculty ranks. Unquestionably, this kind of analysis falls short of the information needed to assist administrators and policy makers in addressing these issues.

On the other hand, it is imperative that academics move beyond the all-too-familiar rationales and excuses of being unable to find "qualified minority" candidates or unable to attract faculty of color because they cannot pay them salaries competitive with other employment sectors. Opp and Smith (1992) found that many attitudinal and structural barriers that hamper recruitment and retention of full-time faculty of color in four-year institutions also hinder their employment at two-year campuses. According to their survey results, structural barriers—that is, economic constraints—were found to be a greater hindrance to minority faculty recruitment than attitudinal barriers in two-year colleges. However, their study also showed that the single best predictor for the increased representation of minority faculty on a campus was having an African American or Hispanic American as vice-president of academic affairs. Representation of persons of color on the board of trustees and the higher employment rate of minority faculty showed a similar correlation. These findings strongly support the notion that the attitude, commitment, and actions of senior level administrators and board members may be a larger mitigating factor in the underrepresentation of two-year minority faculty than many faculty and administrators want to admit.

First, and perhaps foremost, institutional leaders must be committed to employing a talented and diverse faculty, because to push for real change in the arena requires much more than rhetoric about the problem or about why qualified candidates cannot be found. Leaders must understand that continuous and sustained efforts are needed, and they must be willing to hold faculty and other administrators accountable for being part of the solution and not the problem. Successful faculty diversity initiatives are comprehensive, aimed at increasing the future supply and employment of scholars of color, interwoven into the fabric of the institutional culture, and reflected in all policy decisions.

Institutionally based and state-based initiatives that address minority faculty pipeline issues, as well as programs that promote the recruitment of minority scholars, must be expanded. Carter and Wilson (1992) state that successful strategies to increase faculty of color consist of at least three independent components. First, colleges and universities must work to increase the number of graduate degrees awarded to U.S. ethnic minority citizens and find additional ways to interest new master's and doctoral degree recipients of color in academic careers. Community colleges can develop teaching assistantships for minority graduate students recruited from regional colleges and universities, as well as other minority persons from outside academia who have an expressed interest in college teaching. The Minority Teaching Fellowship Program at Catonsville Community College in Maryland illustrates this type of initiative. "The program aims to provide Catonsville' students with diverse faculty, to infuse new approaches and techniques into current courses, to provide an additional mechanism for recruiting minority faculty members, and to provide an opportunity for persons of color to participate in a one-year program of professional development and training at the college. A faculty mentor is designated for each fellow, who is paid a full salary and benefits, serves on campus committees, teaches regular college courses, and can be considered for permanent faculty appointments when positions become available" (Green, 1989, p. 92).

Second, faculty and administrators must examine assumptions in the hiring process that may unfairly eliminate candidates of color from the pool of "qualified" applicants. One of the most persistent and damaging obstacles to employing more faculty of color is the belief among white faculty that educational standards of quality and excellence are invariably compromised by pressures to hire minority faculty. Veiled racism, moral standards of judgment, inexperience with cultural differences, and the failure to fully accept responsibility for identifying and nurturing talent often lie at the bottom of the "best-qualified arguments" (Wilson, 1989). Achieving increased representation of minority faculty requires institutional leaders who recognize that many faculty and administrators are content with the current scenario, and that their efforts must be both "affirmative and proactive" if they are to employ and retain more faculty of color. Efforts to recruit and retain faculty of color must be seen as central to the mission and success of each department, not as an add-on. Incentives for hiring faculty of color should be used in tandem with monitoring each department's performance in diversifying their faculties. The affirmative action officer should be actively involved in the decision-making process in all faculty searches. When hiring pools are not racially or ethnically diverse, strong consideration should be given to reconstituting these searches.

Third, once hired, minority faculty must be retained. Faculty of color, like other faculty, must be supported and mentored to achieve success. All too often they find themselves isolated, working with little support and high service expectations. Departments must guard against expecting faculty of color to assume inordinately high shares of the "caretaking responsibilities" within the department. Additionally, these contributions must be recognized and rewarded as an important part of the tenure and promotion system.

In summary, reversing the inadequate participation of people of color in faculty and leadership positions in higher education is an affirmative action of monumental importance to the future of this nation. One University of Wisconsin official stated:

> In any great and difficult endeavor, there is the temptation to believe that the solution lies elsewhere, is known to others, is new, is magical, and is nearly, if not completely, out of reach. Embracing the value of expanding opportunities for African-Americans and other minorities in higher education begins with the acknowledgement that there is no magic bullet, here or elsewhere, that the solutions—such that they are—are numerous, generally available if desired, rather familiar, and decidedly imperfect. They are, in fact, the same solutions available for solving most public policy problems.

At least to this author, the real problem is not the availability of solutions but the scarcity of commitment to change.

References

Astin, A. W., Korn, W. S., and Dey, E. L. *The American College Teacher: National Norms for the 1989–90 HERI Faculty Survey.* Los Angeles: Higher Education Research Institute, University of California, 1991.

Carter, D. J., and Wilson, R. *1991 Tenth Annual Status Report on Minorities in Higher Education.* Washington, D.C.: American Council on Education, 1992.

Cohen, A. M., and Brawer, F. B. *The American Community College.* (2nd ed.) San Francisco: Jossey-Bass, 1989.

El-Khawas, E. *Campus Trends.* Washington, D.C.: American Council on Education, 1989, 1990, 1991, 1992, and 1993.

Green, M. F. *Minorities on Campus: A Handbook for Enhancing Diversity.* Washington, D.C.: American Council on Education, 1989.

Higher Education Research Institute, University of California, Los Angeles. "1989–90 Higher Education Research Institute Faculty Survey." Unpublished tabulations. November 1991 and March 1992.

O'Brien, E. M. "American Indians in Higher Education." *Research Briefs,* 1992, 3 (3).

O'Hare, W. P. "America's Minorities—The Demographics of Diversity." *Population Bulletin,* December 1992, 47 (4). Washington, D.C.: Population Reference Bureau, Inc.

Opp, R. D., and Smith, A. B. "Minority Faculty Recruitment Programs at Two-Year Colleges." Paper presented at the annual meeting of the American Association of Community and Junior Colleges, 1992.

U.S. Department of Education, National Center for Education Statistics. *Faculty in Higher Education Institutions, 1988: National Survey of Postsecondary Faculty (NSOPF-88).* Washington, D.C.: U.S. Department of Education, Office of Educational Research and Improvement, 1990.

U.S. Department of Education, National Center for Education Statistics. *Trends in Enrollment in Higher Education by Racial/Ethnic Category: Fall 1980 Through Fall 1991.* Washington, D.C.: U.S. Department of Education, 1993.

U.S. Equal Employment Opportunity Commission. EEOC-6 Higher Education Staff Information Survey, 1981 and 1991.

Wilson, R. "Effective Strategies and Programs to Increase Minority Faculty." Paper prepared for the Office of Minority Equity, Lansing, Michigan, 1989.

DEBORAH J. CARTER *is acting director of the Office of Minorities in Higher Education, American Council on Education, Washington, D.C.*

The representation of African American faculty can influence the behavior of an institution and facilitate the kind of climate that would positively influence their retention and future recruitment.

African American Faculty in Community Colleges: Why They Aren't There

William B. Harvey

Community colleges, in many ways, have duplicated the behavior of their brother and sister institutions, the four-year colleges and universities. With less of their own sense of tradition to follow, two-year institutions have adopted many of the practices and procedures used by four-year institutions of higher education, unfortunately with sometimes similar results. For example, the drastic underrepresentation of African American faculty in four-year colleges and universities is also evident in the community colleges. Given that substantial numbers of African American students who attend institutions of higher education are enrolled in community colleges, and that a heightened sensitivity to diversity has emerged throughout the country within the past few years, expressions of concern about the absence of African American faculty members on community college campuses can be heard with great regularity. Nevertheless, hiring and retention patterns continue to show that African Americans are not gaining access to faculty positions at community colleges, particularly at institutions that serve predominantly white student bodies.

Like the four-year colleges and universities, community colleges have reflected the value orientations of the larger society, and as a result, some of the same exclusionary practices have been put to use in both kinds of institutions. The historical legacy of racial discrimination continues to make its presence felt in American society, and the manifestations of this invidious practice, in both overt and covert ways, can be seen in both individual and institutional patterns of behavior and action. In the 1960s, during the "golden era" of higher education when community colleges grew rapidly, Hawthorne observed that "little time was available to mobilize extensive formal search efforts because haste was a feature of the hiring process" (1993, p. 406). Though accurate records of hiring by race do not exist for that particular period of growth and expansion, the community colleges as a cohort hardly distinguished themselves in regards to the employment rate of African Americans as faculty members.

Whether due to the hasty manner of selecting faculty or to attitudinal considerations, the profile of community college faculty members hired during this period was not dissimilar from the faculty profile at the four-year colleges and universities. In both cases, the "typical" faculty member was white and male. In the 1970s, enrollments in the community colleges dropped a bit before stabilizing so fewer employment opportunities were available for aspirants to the faculty. Enrollments began to grow again in the 1980s and early 1990s, but the increasing number of faculty slots that became available in community colleges during this period did not result in substantial numbers of African Americans moving into faculty positions. From 1953 to 1987, the number of two-year college faculty members grew from 23,762 to 256,236 (Cohen and Brawer, 1977, 1989), but even with that phenomenal increase in the number of positions, at present African Americans are estimated to occupy only about 4 percent of these slots (Astin, Korn, and Dey, 1991).

Even during previous periods of expansion then, community colleges were not hiring representative numbers of African Americans as faculty members. As a result, in most institutions African Americans have rarely been able to establish a "critical mass" within the faculty ranks; consequently, they have been able to exert little influence, and even less power, inside the community colleges. The tendency that both two- and four-year predominantly white institutions have to marginalize African American faculty is countered, to some degree, when their numbers are representative and go beyond one or two persons on a campus. But, one of the most frequently heard reasons for African Americans not being hired for vacant faculty positions has been that so few have the appropriate qualifications for an academic appointment. In regards to four-year institutions, the validity of the commonly used expression "We can't find any," in reference to the paucity of suitable African American candidates, has been called into question (Harvey and Scott-Jones, 1985).

In community colleges where, generally speaking, the master's degree is considered sufficient preparation for a faculty appointment, a question first raised in four-year institutions could be similarly posed: whether "We can't find any" might be interpreted to mean "We don't want any" (Harvey and Scott-Jones, 1985).

Table 2.1 indicates that during the past two decades, a pool of African Americans who had earned their master's degrees did exist; thus the supposed scarcity of qualified applicants does not seem a credible explanation. Though these individuals had received educational preparation appropriate for a faculty appointment, in every year identified below, the percentage of African Americans who earned master's degrees was higher than the estimated percentage of African Americans employed as faculty members in community colleges.

Table 2.1. Master's Degree Conferred by Racial Group,
1976–77 to 1990–91

	Total Number of Master's Degree Recipients	Number of African American Recipients	Percentage of African American Recipients
1976–77	316,602	21,037	6.6
1977–78	300,255	19,418	6.5
1980–81	294,183	17,133	5.8
1984–85	280,421	13,939	4.9
1986–87	289,341	13,867	4.8
1988–89	309,770	14,096	4.6
1989–90	322,465	15,446	4.8
1990–91	328,645	16,136	4.9

Source: Astin, Korn, and Dey, 1991.

Academic Culture

To the uninformed, Birnbaum's warning that "American colleges and universities are the most paradoxical of organizations" (1988, p. 3) might seem overstated, but it really is not. One of the ironies of the academic structure is its ability to be perceived as an agent of transition and change. This perception is neither verified by data regarding the relationship between academe and the larger society nor shown in terms of its own operation and function. Higher education devoutly adheres to the maintenance of the status quo.

Perhaps the best example of the academic establishment's timidity in embracing social change is the fact that the nation's colleges and universities generally took no position on the civil rights movement until goaded to do so by student activists. Even in a situation where there was a glaring contradiction between the nation's stated goals of justice and equality and its actions of discrimination and prejudice, the sanctity of the established order appeared to be more important to academic institutions than was society's fair treatment of all its citizens (Harvey, 1991). The academic response to such a situation offers a stark contrast to the possibility of an internal academic modification, such as the notion of expanding the curriculum to provide a more accurate sense of the contributions of all groups to the development of our world. This prospect is met with passionate resistance and agitated verbiage from the stalwart guardians of tradition.

Faculty members, who operate at the core of the institution, tend to select others who share their academic and personal experiences, their value orientations, and their outlooks, to join them. Despite the scarcity of African Americans in faculty positions, incumbent faculty would contend that the outcome of any search is not predetermined and that the recruitment process is constructed to ensure the widest possible range of candidates. According to Hawthorne (1993, p. 407), "recruitment involves the policies and procedures of colleges to attract and select the most qualified instructional staff." Qualifications can be specific and identifiable, such as the receipt of a master's degree, or they can be vague and imprecise, such as the capacity to work well in a collegial setting. As do four-year colleges and universities, community colleges routinely use hiring procedures that result in new faculty members whose racial backgrounds are the same as the individuals responsible for their selection from the candidates considered.

While Reeves and Galant (1986) contend that formal recruitment plans are not commonly used in community colleges, some reasonably well-developed programs can be identified. Whether the faculty hiring that has occurred in community colleges has been carried out by faculty members, administrators, or both, African Americans have rarely been identified as the most qualified candidates for positions; consequently the number of African Americans in the faculty ranks remains at its low level. Although there is insufficient concrete evidence to impute this continued exclusion to racial bias, Gillett-Karam (1993) implies a connection between the absence of African American faculty in the community colleges and the fact that few community college presidents, vice-presidents, or deans are members of minority groups who thus would presumably be more concerned than their white counterparts about having a diverse faculty. This is an important observation because administrative leadership has frequently been identified as one of the important elements in facilitating faculty diversity. On a related note, Amey and Twombly (1992) have pointed out that in community colleges, the images of leadership that have been developed and applauded have tended to perpetuate the great-man (white) model of leadership, a model which may consequently perpetuate the patterns of exclusion of African Americans, in both faculty and administrative positions.

From Presence to Power

Most academicians would certainly want to assume that the underrepresentation of African American faculty should not be ascribed to overt racist behavior on the part of the persons who are involved in faculty selection activities. However, other seemingly benign considerations, such as group affinity and cultural identification, might be seen as covert factors that are less objectionable in making a determination about who should occupy a faculty position. African Americans face a fundamental problem because their lack of representation in the academy makes it more difficult for them to be involved in the decision-making processes as additional or replacement faculty are hired. In other words, the small numbers of African American faculty contribute to the minimalization of their clout as a group, which reduces the degree to which they can be successful advocates for making the institutions more amenable to recruiting and retaining additional African Americans.

Figure 2.1 represents the way in which African American faculty can influence the behavior of an institution and facilitate the kind of climate that would lean toward increasing an African American presence on a community

Figure 2.1. Stages of Impact for African American Faculty

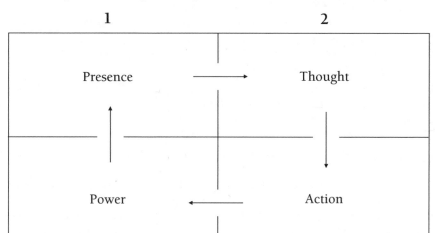

college campus. For African American faculty to have an impact on a community college, there must first be a presence established of one or more members from this group.

American society is so race-conscious that even a single African American on the faculty has an impact on the institution. For European Americans, an African American presence brings to the forefront the underlying tension between fairness and prejudice—the implicit dichotomy that is the "American dilemma"—thus making what is otherwise an interesting philosophical contradiction into a real-life issue that must be confronted and resolved. The larger the African American presence on a given community college campus, the greater the potential impact of this particular group on the institution (section 1). As group members identify their perspectives, outlooks, considerations and concerns to the campus, an intellectual and experiential line is crossed (section 2) and the campus is enriched by having introduced into the institutional environment a set of thoughts/ideas/observations that would have otherwise not been available. Conversely, where there are no African American faculty members, there can be no input into the institutional mix that is authentically reflective of the African American experience.

The next stage of impact for African American faculty occurs when they initiate action on matters that fall within the academic domain and are of personal concern to them. The central role and function played by faculty in the academic setting places them in a unique position to initiate action that will benefit the students and the institution. Indeed, it is the faculty who hold the power to modify fundamental operational aspects of their colleges, including admissions standards, curriculum offerings, and faculty hiring processes (Harvey, 1991). By taking action (section 3), African American faculty challenge the community college to operationalize its stated ideals, while also modifying the existing state of affairs to make the institutional climate more receptive to attracting additional African American faculty. In a direct sense, questions regarding African American faculty underrepresentation can be raised and approaches suggested regarding the search processes used by the institution, expected future faculty vacancies, posting and advertising methods, and outreach efforts to historically black colleges as a means of attracting potential African Americans to join the college faculty. Other kinds of actions that are frequently undertaken by such individuals concern such matters as curriculum reform (particularly the representation of African American studies in the curriculum), provision of adequate advising and counseling services for African American students, and identification of other African Americans to serve as resource persons and mentors for students.

At the point that concrete positive responses are realized as a direct result of their efforts, African American faculty can be considered to be exercising power within the institution (section 4). The most significant manifestation of that power would be seen in increased numbers of African American faculty members being brought into the community college. As the cohort of African American faculty members increases in size, the pattern of activity is repeated, and the institution becomes more responsive to the group. The degree of power that can be accrued by a cohort of African American faculty has a practical limit. At some point, countervailing factors that inhibit actions that the group might want to occur will come into play. Successful completion of some actions, other than increasing the numbers of African American faculty, might indicate gains in power or might represent a compromise between the request made by African American faculty and initial offerings made by the college administration. Economic considerations, for example, might limit the number of courses offered in African American studies, but in turn, the courses could be made part of the college general education program, which would allow students to count them as part of their requirements rather than as electives.

An Institutional Priority

"As the community college in the United States turns ninety years old, the state of preparation, screening and selection of faculty is sporadic, ad hoc, and loosely tied to the needs of the institutions and their students" (Hawthorne, 1993, p. 407). It is not possible to dictate faculty selection from the outside; institutions must take the responsibility to provide a diverse professorial force for their students. The utilization of African Americans among the faculty is an important benefit for a community college to provide its students with an opportunity to learn from and interact with individuals who present a perspective and background that is different from that of the European American instructors. Demographic realities make it clear that America is more diverse now than ever before, and the trend will increase as we move into the twenty-first century.

Whether done through processes that are coordinated by the faculty or by the administration, community colleges must work diligently to make their campus climates hospitable to African American faculty so that African American faculty can fulfill their professional obligations in the most effective and efficient manner, and so that they can, in turn, make their fullest contributions to the institutions. The impediments that have kept African Americans underrepresented among the faculty of community colleges, whether structural or individual, must be removed. Specific steps that might be taken include developing workshops to assist search committees in reaching out to African American candidates in ways they might not have known about or considered before; offering racial sensitivity sessions to provide an understanding of actions, behaviors, or speech that could be offensive to African Americans; and bringing African Americans from various walks of life to the community college, both to share information and to provide a sense of the breadth of the African American experience. Increasing the numbers of African American faculty members in community colleges cannot be an institutional afterthought—it must be an institutional priority. The community colleges must combine their resources with their will in order to be successful in this endeavor.

References

Amey, M., and Twombly, S. "Re-Visioning Leadership in Community Colleges." *Review of Higher Education*, 1992, *15* (2), 125–150.

Astin, A., Korn, W., and Dey, E. *The American College Teacher: National Norms for the 1989–90 HERI Faculty Survey*. Los Angeles: Higher Education Research Institute, University of California, 1991.

Birnbaum, R. *How Colleges Work: The Cybernetics of Academic Organization and Leadership*. San Francisco: Jossey-Bass, 1991.

Cohen, A. M., and Brawer, F. B. *The Two-Year College Instructor Today*. New York: Praeger, 1977.

Cohen, A. M., and Brawer, F. B. *The American Community College*. (2nd ed.) San Francisco: Jossey-Bass, 1989.

Gillett-Karam, R. "Maxims for Excellence in Teaching: Reaching the Underserved." In G. Baker (ed.), *A Handbook on the Community College in America*. Westport, Conn.: Greenwood Press, 1993.

Harvey, W. "Faculty Responsibility and Racial Tolerance." *Thought and Action*, 1991, *8* (2), 43–56.

Harvey, W., and Scott-Jones, D. "We Can't Find Any: The Elusiveness of Black Faculty Members in American Higher Education." *Issues in Education*, 1985, *3* (1), 68–76.

Hawthorne, E. "The Preparation, Screening and Selection of Community College Faculty Members." In G. Baker (ed.), *A Handbook on the Community College in America*. Westport, Conn.: Greenwood Press, 1993.

Reeves, R., and Galant. R. *An Academic Resource in Low Supply and High Demand: A Survey of Community College Recruitment Plans of General Education Faculty Over the Next Five Years*, 1986. (ED 273 334)

WILLIAM B. HARVEY is professor of higher education, adult and community college education, North Carolina State University, Raleigh.

The California Community Colleges have implemented a plan to achieve a full-time faculty and staff work force that reflects the adult population of the state by the year 2005.

California Community College Faculty from Historically Underrepresented Racial and Ethnic Groups

Dorothy M. Knoell

California's Historic Commitment

California's rapidly changing racial and ethnic mix scarcely needs to be recounted here, except perhaps for the observation that there will soon be no "majority" group. While the population continues to increase, middle-class white citizens are leaving the state and immigrants from other countries—predominantly Latino and Asian—outnumber citizens moving to California from other states. Implications for the state's future work force are overwhelming, given the needs of these new Californians for education and services.

The commitment of the California Community Colleges to affirmative action, diversity, and educational equity dates back to the late 1960s—when the legislature established the state-level Board of Governors for what has become a system of more than 100 two-year colleges that serve as many as one and one half million students each year. In 1969, not long after the Board began functioning, the legislature enacted into statute the Community College Extended Opportunity Programs and Services (EOPS) that provides financial and academic support with these objectives: increasing access to the colleges for low-income, educationally challenged, and racially/ethnically underrepresented students; and enhancing their persistence and academic success in the colleges. While membership in an underrepresented group is not a requirement for participation in the program, EOPS students are predominantly (69 percent) from racial and ethnic groups that have been historically underrepresented in higher education.

Almost 20 years later, the legislature enacted an omnibus community college reform bill into statute that, among other provisions, expressed the near-term goal of achieving a 39 percent systemwide full-time hiring rate of underrepresented racial/ethnic groups during 1992–93, and a long-term goal of achieving a systemwide full-time work force that reflects the adult population of the state in the year 2005. This section of the legislation acknowledged the finding that the colleges' success in recruiting and hiring black, Latino, Asian, and Native American personnel had failed to match their commitment—and was less successful—than their recruitment and retention of EOPS students.

The statute and the Board's commitment spring from legislative findings and declarations that many benefits are to be derived from a college work force that is reflective of the demographic composition of the state. Benefits include:

The educationally sound impact of the positive image provided to all community college students by minority representatives in the college work force;
The institutionally beneficial perception of community colleges being welcoming, comprehensively diverse organizations;
The societally rewarding effect of implicit lessons concerning democratic principles and inclusiveness that can be best taught through diverse populations working toward common goals.

The sections that follow will describe the legislation that established the agenda for achieving diversity in the community college work force, the implementation of the statutory programs and requirements, and the results to date. Finally, acknowledgement of problems and challenges that persist will be covered. While the statute deals with the entire full-time work force in the community college, the remainder of the chapter will focus on the faculty.

Actions to Increase Faculty Diversity

A variety of strategies underscores the California Community Colleges' commitment to faculty diversity. Leadership, rewards and incentives, an Affirmative Action job fair, and accountability are all key components.

Leadership from the top. Leadership from the top—the Board of Governors and the Chancellor's Office—has been an essential ingredient of the state's commitment to increase diversity in the colleges' work force, accompanied by local responsiveness. While the majority of their funding has come from the state since Proposition 13, which limited local property taxes, was passed, community colleges continue to be governed by locally elected boards. These boards differ in their willingness to comply with state regulations and guidelines when they are unlikely to incur fiscal penalties for noncompliance. Thus in the area of affirmative action and the achievement of diversity—where local autonomy and differences in community characteristics may be offered as grounds for noncompliance—leadership is necessary but not sufficient for success.

Leadership from the top is exemplified by the Board of Governors Equity, Diversity, and Human Resources Committee, staffed by a vice-chancellor and dean for a Human Resources Division, together with a staff of specialists for the many areas in which the division has responsibility. In addition, the chancellor works with a Task Force on Equity, Diversity, and Development that has a broad-based membership of 23 persons from the field and meets six times a year. This is the only such task force with which the chancellor works directly.

Rewards and incentives. Because leadership without rewards and incentives may be ineffective, the California program has both. Rewards are actually awards presented by the Board of Governors to college districts and to individuals who have made outstanding contributions toward the goal of achieving ethnic, gender, and disability representation in staffing. Districts receive awards for having the highest diversity hiring rates and the most diverse staff, while individual award winners are chosen by affirmative action consortia.

Incentives are provided from the Faculty and Staff Diversity Fund, from which grants are awarded to districts on a competitive basis for extended outreach and recruitment, incentive to hire, inservice training, and other purposes that promote staff diversity. Grants are made to colleges for proposals designed to facilitate the development of model programs which encourage faculty and staff diversity in the colleges. Proposals for the 1992–1993 grants were required to contain one or more of the following prioritized elements: (1) model selection procedures that lead to greater faculty and staff diversity; (2) programs aimed at retaining new and existing employees from underrepresented groups; (3) methods of recruiting faculty and staff from underrepresented groups; (4) methods of mentoring diverse staff into the community college system; and (5) inservice activities that sensitize faculty and staff to the need for diversity and result in the same. Still another type of (negative) recognition is given to colleges in the lowest quartile—ranked by their hiring rates. Those in this category receive technical assistance from the chancellor's office staff on how to improve their rates of hiring from underrepresented groups. Experience to date has shown that those in the bottom quartile tend to be the smallest colleges.

Affirmative Action plans. District plans are updated from the late 1980s to comply with recent revisions in regulations. They were to be submitted to the chancellor's office by July 1, 1993, but the issue of reimbursement by the state for developing or updating these plans (now resolved) has delayed expected compliance. Meanwhile, all districts had submitted acceptable plans under the old regulations that included goals and timetables. Now, districts are being asked to report on an assessment of where they are in affirmative action hiring (baseline information) and to have their updated plans ready by the end of the calendar year.

Advertising and registry. One of the state programs that the Chancellor's Office and others fund is the annual California Community Colleges Affirmative Action Job Fair that was first held in 1989. It is advertised in various national publications, such as *The Chronicle of Higher Education* and *Change*

Magazine, and is held in several central locations. This year colleges from Washington, Oregon, Utah, Iowa, and Florida, as well as the California colleges, have participated in the fair. The project has not undergone a formal evaluation of its effectiveness in increasing or facilitating the recruitment of the targeted faculty and staff, but opinions about the activities seem to have generally been positive.

Accountability. The Community College Reform Act of 1988 requires the Board of Governors to report to the legislature annually "regarding the number of districts which have adopted and are maintaining affirmative action programs, including the effectiveness of such programs." The most recent report (January 1993) reviews the latest full-time work force diversity statistics, including systemwide trends and differences among colleges in affirmative action efforts, and summarizes efforts that have been undertaken pursuant to diversity goals and "some of the intrinsic challenges."

The report includes two major categories of data that are related to the near- and long-term goals. The first is "hiring rates"—a measure of the incremental changes in the composition of the work force that are related to the near-term goal of a 30 percent hiring rate of individuals from underrepresented racial/ethnic groups. The second is "staffing rates"—a measure that reflects the composition of the entire work force, rather than simply new hires. Staffing rates are related to the long-term staffing goals for the year 2005, that the work force reflect the racial/ethnic composition of the adult population of California.

Effectiveness of the Programs

The chancellor's office staff reached the general conclusion from data showing changes during the three-year period, Fall 1988 to Fall 1991, that the Faculty and Staff Diversity program "is effectively working towards the goals of the Legislature [and the Board of Governors]." In other words, the near-term goal of 30 percent new hires from underrepresented groups had been reached and exceeded by the year 1992–93. However, the staff was less positive in evaluating progress toward the long-term goal of a work force that resembles the adult population, pointing out that "when the complexities of the situation are portrayed, full realization of the long-term diversity goal may be difficult."

As noted earlier, the California Community College affirmative action program includes all levels and types of full-time personnel that the colleges employ. Furthermore, the 1993 report to the Legislature deals first of all with changes between Fall 1990 and Fall 1991 because the provision of monetary and technical assistance to the college districts in 1989 was too late to have a major impact before that period. The hiring rate for faculty between Fall 1990 and Fall 1991 was above 30 percent (31.2 percent), but it was lower than the rates for executive/administrative/management (36.4 percent), professional non-faculty (33.0 percent), clerical (33.3 percent), and service/maintenance personnel (49.9 percent). It exceeded only technical/paraprofessional staff

(30.6 percent) and skilled craftspersons (27.2 percent). For faculty alone, the mean hiring rate for the 18 community college districts in the top quartile was 38.8 percent, while the mean for the lowest quartile was 23.2 percent during that period. The smallest colleges, with few opportunities to hire new staff in recent years, tended to be in the lowest quartile—with exceptions such as Compton College, whose students are black or Latino and which had a three-year minority faculty hiring rate of 80 percent.

It is not surprising to find differences among the disciplines in Fall 1991 in the statewide hiring rates for various racial/ethnic groups. Of those areas with at least 50 new hires that fall, foreign languages displayed the highest rate—62.0 percent, 40 percent of whom were Latino. Two others with "minority" hiring rates above 30 percent were social sciences (34.7 percent, drawing from all underrepresented groups except Native American), and mathematics (31.5 percent, drawing heavily upon Asian candidates). Humanities/letters employed the largest number of new full-time faculty that fall (238), 29.0 percent of whom were from underrepresented groups. The largest numbers of Filipino, Latino, and Native Americans and the second largest number of Asians were hired in this category.

The disciplines with the lowest hiring rates for underrepresented groups were education (13.2 percent), fine and applied arts (18.0 percent), engineering and related technologies (18.6 percent), and health (18.7 percent). In the fields identified above, more than 75 new full-time faculty were hired for the term. New Latino faculty were the largest underrepresented racial/ethnic group to be hired full-time in Fall 1991 (137 individuals, or 10.3 percent of the total new hires), followed by Asian (112, or 8.4 percent). Only 12 new hires were black (1.0 percent), 25 Native American (1.9 percent), and 68 Filipino (5.0 percent), with white faculty comprising the remaining 73.3 percent of the new hires.

Finally, the 1993 report to the legislature included trend data for the eight-year period beginning Fall 1994. Overall an increase of 7.9 percent was reported in the hiring of new, full-time faculty. The largest numerical change was reported for Latino faculty—an increase of 418 to 1,245, a 50.5 percent increase. The largest percentage increase was for Native Americans, the second smallest group, which experienced a 60.6 percent increase of 57 positions to bring the total to 151, followed by Asian faculty with 275 new positions for a total of 774, or a 55.1 percent increase. Black faculty increased 25.5 percent or 195 positions to a total of 959, while Filipino faculty increased 42.6 percent or 20 positions to total 67 in all. White faculty increased only 2.0 percent or 266 positions during the same period and decreased their representation from 85.7 to 81.0 percent of the new full-time faculty hires. Viewed still another way, 78.4 percent of the new faculty hires during the eight-year period were members of underrepresented racial/ethnic groups, thus moving the colleges slowly but with some confidence toward the long-term goal of having the faculty reflect the racial/ethnic composition of the state's adult population.

Persistent Problems and Challenges

The most immediate hindrance to achieving affirmative action goals for faculty hiring is the strong competition among California's colleges and universities for a limited pool of qualified applicants from historically underrepresented groups for faculty openings—competition that is exacerbated by recruitment from the same pool by institutions in other states. The problem begins with low rates of eligibility for freshman admission to California's public universities for black and Latino high school graduates, together with low rates of persistence to graduation for those who enter as freshman, and finally, low rates of enrollment in graduate school to prepare for teaching. The challenge is, therefore, to increase high school graduation rates and preparation for college among these youth, accompanied by assistance in securing admission and financial aid that is necessary to meet the ever-increasing cost of attendance, and then to recruit them into preparation for teaching at the community college level. The California colleges no longer require that faculty members be credentialed or hold a master's degree in the discipline, but they continue to be hindered by strong competition for a limited pool of candidates.

A lack of openings for new full-time faculty members is an increasing problem for the California colleges, which are under conditions of both budget cuts and uncertainty about enrollment levels in the near future as fees continue to increase. Colleges have experienced enrollment losses in 1992–93 that have not been accompanied by faculty attrition, one result of which is a lack of vacancies into which to hire faculty from underrepresented groups.

Locally established salary scales under collective bargaining procedures constitute both a problem and a challenge. The problem results when some colleges that offer high salaries are able to recruit from colleges with low faculty salary scales, thus reducing the chances of achieving statewide affirmative action goals. Other conditions that differ among the colleges also affect recruitment. Such factors as geographic remoteness, size, racial/ethnic composition of the college and its service area, focus of the college mission, and proximity to a university affect a potential faculty member's—and his or her family's—perceived quality of life. The challenge beyond recruitment is to achieve a good match between new faculty and the college at which they will teach and the community in which they will live, in order to retain them when alternative employment offers come their way.

Community colleges continue to enroll a large majority of the black and Latino youth who go to college anywhere in California, but their success is poor in both retaining and then transferring them to universities to obtain baccalaureate degrees that might prepare them for college teaching. Any significant shift by black and Latino freshman from community colleges to the universities in the near term seems unlikely, given the steep increases in university fees that have occurred during the state's persistent fiscal crisis. The immediate challenge to the community colleges is then to increase dramatically the persistence, performance, and transfer of students from historically under-represented racial/ethnic groups, with the goal of recruiting larger numbers into community college teaching positions.

References

Board of Governors, California Community Colleges. *Affirmative Action Programs in the California Community Colleges, 1991–92: An Annual Report to the Board of Governors and Legislature.* Sacramento: Chancellor's Office, January 1993.

Board of Governors, California Community Colleges. *1993–94, Expenditure Plan: Faculty and Staff Diversity Grants.* Sacramento: Chancellor's Office, January 1993.

Board of Governors, California Community Colleges. *Annual Report: Matriculation and Extended Opportunity Programs and Services.* Sacramento: Chancellor's Office, March 1993.

California Legislature. Assembly Bill 1725, Community College Reform Bill, (Education Code Chapter 1973, Statutes of 1988).

Chancellor's Office, California Community Colleges. *Communique,* Periodic Newsletter. Sacramento: Chancellor's Office, Division of Human Resources.

DOROTHY M. KNOELL *is chief policy analyst for the California Postsecondary Education Commission, Sacramento.*

Three decades after the beginning of the civil rights movement, community colleges still lack an adequate minority faculty presence on their campuses. Changes to promote diversity will require awareness, leadership, dialogue and long-range planning.

Achieving Diversity Among Community College Faculty

Freddie W. Nicholas, Sr., Arnold R. Oliver

A thirty-year struggle, filled with shouting and demagoguery, charges and countercharges, has failed to lessen the deeply felt controversy surrounding affirmative action and the achievement of diversity on community college campuses. Remaining in the hearts and minds of many are serious doubts about one of the most complex and misunderstood social policies ever adopted. Today's multiplicity of meanings and the polemics that surround affirmative action make it nearly impossible to agree on what the commitment to diversity means.

History and Rhetoric of Diversity

The historical perspective of this thirty-year war offers a view of progress in a sense, yet it suggests that the issue is far from simply fading into the night. The mid-1960s bore the first ripening fruits of the civil rights movement. A painful and slow progress occurred, progress characterized by continual debate and enough paper to circle the globe. The period was marked with anger, shame, and hostility. Nonetheless, some progress occurred. In 1961, less than one percent of all faculty at predominantly white institutions was African American. With significant pressure from the federal courts, some institutions began to change. By 1979 African Americans represented 2.3 percent of the faculty at predominantly white institutions (Carter and Wilson, 1992, p. 20). Despite seemingly lackluster advances in the representation of minority and female faculty and administrators in America's colleges and universities, the changes of the 1960s were significant. The significance lies in the awareness that developed during the decade of intrinsic wrong-mindedness of systematic, de jure exclusionary laws and policies and the destructiveness of such policies. The role of Congress, the president, and the federal courts were critical in creating an atmosphere where these issues were explored more fully than ever before in our history.

Issues relating to diversity remained visible and controversial through the 1980s. Controversies were based on the volatile notion that quotas were in place to allow women and minorities, no matter what their qualifications, to be hired over more qualified white males. People knew that quotas existed and recognized the unfairness in an action to hire an individual unqualified for a position. The hiring of an unqualified individual not only condemns the person to failure but reinforces many of the dehumanizing stereotypes within our society. Books and publications urged our sensitivity to these issues, and community colleges and universities continued to demand greater commitment to minorities and women.

The debates of the past three decades show some areas of substantial progress. For example, impassioned pleas to justify salary differences for men and women doing the same task are now rare. Seldom is the notion argued that public institutions and organizations will be forever destroyed if they cannot retain their gender, racial, or ethnic exclusivity. On the other hand, it seems that minorities and women are in more visible roles within many community colleges and other institutions of higher education as affirmative action has changed the way many enterprises go about employment.

Despite all efforts, however, Carter and Wilson (1992) report that there is virtually no difference in the percentages of African American faculty at predominantly white institutions today than in 1979. The growth in actual numbers of black faculty has simply kept pace with the growth of all faculty during the decade. The only increases are for African American women in the categories of administration and management—2.9 percent in 1979 increased to 4.2 percent in 1988 (pp. 22–23). As Table 4.1 illustrates, little substantial percentage change has been realized for Hispanics and American Indians.

Some argue that the progress has been at the expense of white males; others argue that the lack of progress has been at the expense of all minorities and women. Some decry the lack of opportunities for minorities; others assert that they have no obligation to correct past inequities, further arguing that enough has already been done.

Despite all the rhetoric, elaborately written plans, data, shelves full of documents, and despite all the protestations of Boards of Trustees, educational leaders, and government officials, the reality is that little progress has occurred for most minorities and women since the mid-1970s. While there has been some increase in the number of minorities hired, it is roughly proportional to the number of new positions in higher education over that same period. African American faculty in higher education represent only about 4.4 percent of all faculty, including faculty at historically black colleges and universities.

Tables 4.2 and 4.3 tell of the basic lack of progress and reflect the inability of institutions to change the reality of their employment patterns. It is

Table 4.1. Full-Time Faculty in Higher Education by Race/Ethnicity and Sex, 1979, 1983, 1985, and 1989

	1979		1983		1985		1989		Percent Change
	Total	%	Total	%	Total	%	Total	%	1979–89
Total	451,348	100.0	485,739	100.0	473,537	100.0	514,662	100.0	14.0
Men	335,295	74.3	356,579	73.4	342,916	72.4	358,562	69.7	6.9
Women	116,053	25.7	129,160	26.5	130,621	27.6	156,100	30.3	34.5
White[a]	410,933	91.0	440,505	90.7	426,468	90.1	455,600	88.5	10.9
Men	308,464	68.3	326,171	65.7	319,018	65.7	319,330	62.0	3.5
Women	102,469	22.7	114,334	29.5	115,450	24.4	136,270	26.5	33.0
African American[b]	19,494	4.3	19,571	4.0	19,559	4.1	23,225	4.5	19.1
Men	10,577	2.3	10,541	2.2	10,631	2.2	12,483	2.4	18.0
Women	8,917	2.0	9,030	1.9	8,928	1.9	10,742	2.1	20.5
Hispanic	6,779	1.5	7,456	1.5	7,788	1.6	10,087	2.0	48.8
Men	4,871	1.1	5,240	1.1	5,458	1.2	6,757	1.3	38.7
Women	1,908	0.4	2,216	0.5	2,330	0.5	3,330	0.6	74.5
Asian American[c]	13,086	2.9	16,899	3.5	18,245	3.9	24,125	4.7	84.4
Men	10,629	2.4	13,677	2.8	14,682	3.1	19,006	3.7	78.8
Women	2,457	0.5	3,222	0.7	3,563	0.8	5,119	1.0	108.3
American Indian[d]	1,056	0.2	1,308	0.3	1,477	0.3	1,408	0.3	41.0
Men	754	0.2	950	0.2	1,127	0.2	986	0.2	30.8
Women	302	0.1	358	0.1	350	0.1	512	0.1	69.5

Note: Details may not add to total due to rounding. Includes full-time faculty in nontenured positions, tenured faculty, and nontenured faculty in tenure-track positions. Figures based on 2,879 institutions in 1979; 3,011 in 1983; 2,856 in 1985; 3, 452 in 1989. Data are based on reported counts and are not input for nonreporting institutions.

[a]White (non-Hispanic)
[b]African American (non-Hispanic)
[c]Asian American (includes Pacific Islanders)
[d]American Indian (includes Alaskan natives)

Source: U.S. Equal Opportunity Commission surveys, "FFO 6 Higher Education Staff Information," 1979, 1983, 1985, 1989.

important for community colleges to understand their unique roles in communities; it is important for individuals comprising the faculty, staff, and administration to feel and to understand the potential impact community colleges have on communities. A critical issue for community colleges is to interpret and articulate their roles in the community. Often described as the greatest egalitarian force in twentieth-century society, community colleges can respond to diversity issues better, more thoughtfully, and more effectively than other segments of higher education. It is important that they do so. To commit to diversity is to endorse the essence of the community college mission: A belief in the potential value of every individual and a commitment to provide educational opportunities, curricula, and creative outreach and support programs without regard to gender, ancestry, or social class.

There are already those who have cast this article aside, saying that it is of no relevance to their situations. There are already those who have shrugged

Table 4.2. Percentage of Full-Time Faculty by Race

	1979	1991
African American	4.3%	4.7%
White	91.3	87.9
Hispanic	2.9	5.1
Asian American	1.5	2.2

Source: U.S. Equal Opportunity Commission.

Table 4.3. Percentage of Full-Time Faculty by Gender

	1979	1991
Women	25.7%	31.8%
Men	74.3%	68.2%
Total number	451,346	520,551

Source: U.S. Equal Employment Commission, Diversity in Community Colleges.

and said that there is nothing else they can do—that they have met all federal and state requirements for affirmative action. There are those who have already rejected, out of hand, their responsibility for any of the multitudes of past or present discriminations. And, yes, there are those who continue to harbor the deep-seated prejudices that continue to pulse through our society.

Too many educational leaders choose to justify the lack of progress instead of taking steps to push diversity forward. The litany of rationalization is so familiar:

There is a lack of available minority and female applicants in the field.
We cannot compete with industry or universities because they pay higher salaries.
Minorities and women are not the best in the pools.
Seeking out any particular kind of individual is wrong.
It hurts everyone when less qualified candidates are hired (a particularly lethal logic that implies all minorities and women are less qualified and less able).
Our students, faculty, boards of trustees, and communities are not ready for this kind of change—it will put our colleges completely out of touch with the power structure of the community.
We hired a minority; he just never fit in.

Yet, some community colleges across our country have made very strong commitments to affirmative action, to changing the institutional culture and patterns of employment, and they have done so with real success. For example, Miami-Dade Community College, Maricopa County College District, Northern Virginia Community College, and Bunker Hill Community College are among those most often cited for their successes. Leaders of these institutions were not simply driven by the fact that their communities may have had a greater diversity, although that clearly has had an impact. The overriding motivation was that it was the right thing to do. These institutions seemed to reject the often used proposition that the institution was working hard on affirmative action but just could not seem to find the people to hire. Hard as it is to imagine, after twenty-five to thirty years of effort, some still suggest a lack of availability as the reason for not employing even one minority faculty member or female administrator.

The Role of the Institutional Leader. The institutions that have been successful in making strides toward real diversity have a single, major distinguishing characteristic that separates them from all others: the leader of the institution has a real belief in diversity. The chancellor or president has made a commitment to increase the numbers of minorities and women at all levels within the institution.

The institutional leader understands the critical role that diversity in higher education plays within our society and the powerful message that diversity transmits to all segments of society. Minorities and women as administrators and faculty are in respected positions. The very fact that they occupy these positions quickly breaks down the stereotypes that foster a continuing prejudice. Whether we have a society that is a melting pot or one that is a salad with distinguishable ingredients, the critical issue is that a pluralistic society needs to have all its members as full participants. To hold important the belief in the American dream and its incumbent values, people must understand that the time for action in higher education is long overdue. Those who refuse responsibility can probably continue to offer the usual explanations for the lack of progress, but they simply delay and make even more painful the coalescing of our society. Without commitment from the top of an institution's structures, and without a vision of how these changes can occur, managers abdicate the responsibility for full diversity within higher education and to the larger society.

The role of leadership cannot be overrated; it is critical to the effort. The top management of the institution must articulate the vision of what can be and clearly communicate the means to achieve the goals toward excellence. Throughout the administrative structure, plans must be designed not simply to protect the institution against charges of discrimination, but to achieve significant progress toward diversity.

Developing Awareness. The call for action is the beginning. Sensitizing the college community to the issues of diversity is far more complicated and time-consuming. The plan may need a series of sensitizing workshops that can help the constituent groups of the college community move beyond denial and defensive argumentation. These take many forms as Gillett-Karam, Roueche, and Roueche (1991) point out, from the single mistake syndrome that one error by a minority or woman is proof that the whole group is not competent, to the "I knew they couldn't do it" mentality (p. 13).

These sessions are hard work; they require the attention and participation of the institution's leader. At times, the discussions should and can lead to redefining the institution's responsibilities which lie beyond instruction and include greater responsibilities to the society.

Clearly the approaches that articulate the commitment and the call for action will vary widely depending on the openness of the institution's culture and the leadership style, but commitment to change and to increasing awareness of needs are the crucial first steps. We rarely deny ourselves the opportunity to raise issues and discussions about the mission and purpose of an institution, yet to initiate discussions about the faculty and administration's view of the value of people and their roles within society seems outlandish at many institutions. Every college should commit to developing a plan of action that exceeds traditional efforts and incorporates broad-based participation in the planning.

These events cannot occur in a week or two. In many cases, the institution must address not only the groups concerned, but also other groups which are clearly threatened and hostile. Formal discussions should create a sense of empowerment among women, minorities, and the persuaded—those who already believe in diversity. This creates a basis for further discussion, albeit painful and argumentative at times, in the lounges and offices of the campuses. Presentations on diversity should lend credibility to further discourse within the institution. The culture changes because individuals, previously isolated and probably silent, have a basis to engage in ongoing dialogue and conversation.

Once the leadership has created a sense of empowerment with the clear message that these issues are important, it is possible to debate the issues within the various groups of the campus. Then the ideas to create diversity can begin to flow and prevent individuals who insist on halting any development in the issues of diversity from holding sway.

Innovative Initiatives. Initiating programs that aggressively seek well-qualified minority candidates and women through wide varieties of networks and personal contacts must be supported and encouraged. Programs focused on identifying, developing, and recruiting minorities and women in graduate schools—and assisting them in financing their graduate education—can be established. Lecture series can be offered to ensure that faculty and staff—and students as well—regularly see role models in a variety of leadership positions. These and other initiatives can provide the impetus for change. And, finally, the president must be willing to commit institutional resources to solutions that enhance institutional diversity.

Hiring Practices. There are a host of possible approaches to expanding the pool of qualified applicants and to creating interview and selection committees that are not dominated by a single point of view. Affirmative action means exactly that—to take positive steps to seek out well-qualified minorities and women. Colleges often insist that interview committees have minority representation and that candidate pools are not finalized until minority and female candidates with the appropriate credentials are found. Often administrators are charged to expand the pools; therefore, they need to develop minority contacts and networks and establish creative and flexible approaches to recruitment. When a vacancy occurs, it is almost too late to begin affirmative action. Rather, it should be continuous, with the new hires of adjunct faculty and staff, with ongoing dialogue and perhaps faculty exchanges with historically black colleges or universities and with business and industry. Creative programs that look at promising undergraduates have significant potential in expanding the applicant pool and also in attracting bright, talented individuals to community colleges.

Dialogue. Meeting the challenge of diversity requires a willingness to engage in dialogue with a variety of constituent groups, some of which may be hostile, cynical, impatient, or simply uninterested. There are considerable risks in undertaking the effort. In fact, a program that is action-oriented and results-driven will at some point cause considerable criticism of the leadership from nearly all quarters. Others will be unhappy with the pace of the change or the perceived weakness or reluctance of the leadership to take large risks, and still others will be critical simply because the institution's equilibrium has been upset.

Long-Range Planning. Beyond immediate, short-term plans, a commitment to work and create a system that encourages minorities and women from elementary school through doctoral programs is a critical piece of long-range vision. We can develop our existing faculty, we can find excellent minorities and women in graduate programs, and we can search our own staffs for capable para-professionals, institutional assistants, lab assistants, and others to develop into faculty and administrators. Communities have individuals who, with encouragement and support for additional education, can become outstanding faculty members and administrators. Support comes in a variety of forms: tuition assistance, flexible scheduling, encouragement, opportunities to attend conferences, to network among professionals in the field, and to find mentors and role models. The stark reality is that we need greater numbers of minorities and women at all stages of the educational process in order to realize substantial long-term progress. It is time to recognize that we must develop a significant partnership with all educational institutions. Developing minority students as potential faculty is essential to a future vision of a day when actions that now seem extraordinary become just a footnote in history.

A plan to create real diversity on a campus should obviously include a commitment to diversity of staff, administrators, faculty, and students. Leadership will require a willingness to avoid playing numbers games. Each plan must look beyond a reflection of the positions traditionally held by women and minorities, such as clerical or custodial jobs. The analysis needs to look beyond those gross measures to assess the people actually in management and faculty positions and avoid playing another game: comparing faculty by race and gender, but mixing full and part-time faculty together. The same point is equally valid in assessing the effectiveness of student diversity programs. Community colleges have had more than enough time to matriculate transfer students and graduates in numbers that at least mirror the community's population base.

It is time for community college administrators who proclaim that affirmative action programs are making a difference to acknowledge that their faculty and staff are no more diverse now than they were in 1980. It is time for colleges who have all-white, all-male administrative staffs to admit that their programs have failed. It is time for community colleges to lead higher education to a new level of democratization, and the centerpiece of that program must be diversity. It is time to shatter the anachronistic values regarding women and minorities. It is time to stop the paternalistic caution that a department, a division, a college, a community, or a region may not be ready for a minority or a woman. There is far less risk in hiring a well-qualified person regardless of gender or ethnicity than there is in continuing the devastating practice of using glass ceilings and other exclusionary devices to keep people out.

Diversity can be achieved and celebrated. Progress requires commitment from leaders and their willingness to take risks, to cause change, to create new institutional cultures. By continuing in our present mode, we ignore the chance to create a solution and leave to the next generations intractable national problems, problems for which solutions are available today.

References

Carter, D. J., and Wilson, R. *Minorities in Higher Education: 1991 Tenth Annual Status Report.* Washington, D.C.: American Council on Education, 1992.

Gillett-Karam, R., Roueche, D., and Roueche, J. E. *Underrepresentation and the Question of Diversity: Women and Minorities in the Community College.* Washington, D.C.: American Association of Community and Junior Colleges, 1991.

FREDDIE W. NICHOLAS, SR., *is president emeritus of John Tyler Community College, Chester, Virginia.*

ARNOLD R. OLIVER *is chancellor of Virginia Community College System in Richmond.*

The results of two surveys of 1,387 two-year college administrators reveal that attitudinal and structural barriers need to be removed before improvements can be made in the percentage of minority full-time faculty at community colleges.

Effective Strategies for Enhancing Minority Faculty Recruitment and Retention

Ronald D. Opp, Albert B. Smith

A recent study reveals that two-year colleges report enrolling a disproportionately large number of minority students, while minority representation among full-time faculty members remains low. In this study, institutional data on the numbers of minority full-time, two-year college faculty are provided, and the types of strategies presently being used by two-year institutions to recruit and retain minority faculty members are discussed in detail. Strategies found to be particularly successful in facilitating the recruitment and retention of minority faculty include hiring minorities to serve as chief academic administrators, hiring minority faculty for ethnic studies departments, having minorities serve on the board of trustees, recruiting minorities from private industry to teach part time, and canceling positions without minority applicants.

Background

Increasing the representation of minorities among full-time faculty is a particularly important issue at the two-year college level. In a current study, two-year colleges were reported to enroll a disproportionately large share of all minority students enrolled in higher education. Fifty-five percent of all Hispanics, 52 percent of all American Indians, and 42 percent of all African Americans enrolled in higher education are attending two-year colleges (U.S. Department of Education, 1992).

The same study reported that minority students accounted for 19.2 percent of the nation's 13.7 million college students in 1990, up from 16.1 percent in 1980. Given this disproportionately large number of minority students enrolled in two-year colleges, the need for minority representation among full-time faculty is particularly critical in this sector. A significant presence of minority full-time faculty may help two-year colleges become more successful in recruiting and retaining minority students.

Minority faculty on two-year college campuses may also help increase the educational aspirations of minority students by providing positive role models of individuals who have achieved high levels of academic success. They may also help white students overcome prejudices about the intellectual capabilities of persons of color and may help white faculty members gain deeper understanding and appreciation for different cultures (Linthicum, 1989). For all of these reasons, adequate representation of minority faculty is essential for excellence as well as equity in two-year colleges.

Federal data on the representation of minorities among full-time faculty in all higher education sectors are readily available. A recent survey reported that African Americans represent 4.5 percent, Hispanics 1.9 percent, and American Indians 0.3 percent of all full-time faculty (U.S. Equal Employment Opportunity Commission, 1990). The representation of these minority groups among full-time faculty is significantly less than their proportional representation in the overall U.S. population within which African Americans make up 12.1 percent, Hispanics 9.0 percent, and American Indians 0.8 percent (U.S. Department of Commerce, 1991). Clearly, African Americans, Hispanics, and American Indians are significantly underrepresented among full-time faculty compared to their representation in the general population.

Because Equal Employment Opportunity Commission (EEOC) data regarding the distribution of faculty by race/ethnicity are typically not reported by institutional type, researchers interested in these distributions within two-year colleges have to rely on sources other than the EEOC. In the most recent national study, based on a weighted sample of faculty in 89 community colleges, Astin, Korn, and Dey (1991) found that about 7.1 percent of full-time, two-year college faculty were members of underrepresented minority groups.

Purpose of the Study

One purpose of this study was to provide current institutional data on the numbers and percentages of underrepresented minorities among full-time, two-year college faculty. Unlike previous studies in which data reported on minority two-year college faculty were based on data gathered indirectly from faculty surveys (Russell, Fairweather, Hendrickson, and Zimbler, 1991; Astin, Korn, and Dey, 1991), this study was based on information gathered directly from two-year colleges. The study permits the comparison of the numbers of minority faculty members reported by colleges with the weighted estimates of the numbers derived from national faculty surveys.

Another purpose of the study was to examine what academic administrators believe are barriers to minority faculty recruitment and retention. A number of researchers have posited specific attitudinal and structural factors that hinder the recruitment and retention of minorities to four-year institutions (Banks, 1984; Bunzel, 1990; Exum, 1983; Exum, Menges, Watkins, and Berglund, 1984; Menges and Exum, 1983; Mickelson and Oliver, 1991; Moore, 1988; Reed, 1983; Reed, 1986, Smelser and Content, 1980). This study was designed to test empirically whether these same attitudinal and structural factors are perceived as barriers to recruiting and retaining minority faculty at two-year colleges as well.

A final purpose of the study was to determine empirically what characterizes successful programs of minority faculty recruitment and retention. Much of the research reported in existing literature has been focused primarily on describing strategies for improving faculty recruitment and retention without testing empirically how successful these strategies actually are. This analysis provides information about which strategies two-year college faculty, administrators, and policy makers can use in designing more effective minority faculty recruitment and retention practices.

Research Design

The study relied on data from two questionnaires received from a total of 1,387 respondents.

Definitions. Underrepresented minorities in this study were defined as those minority groups whose presence among full-time faculty in higher education is not proportionate with their overall representation in the U.S. population. Using this definition of underrepresentation, the investigators focused on four different minority groups: African Americans, Mexican Americans, Puerto-Rican Americans, and American Indians. Full-time faculty was defined as those individuals for whom teaching is the principal activity and who were considered full-time employees at their institutions for at least nine months of the 1991–1992 or 1992–1993 academic years.

Questionnaire Design. The recruitment and retention questionnaire utilized for this study included questions on respondents' demographic backgrounds, campus demographics, barriers to minority faculty recruitment and retention, and recruitment and retention strategies. Individual questions were constructed after a thorough review of the literature and research on minority faculty recruitment and retention. To establish content validity, drafts of the two questionnaires were distributed to faculty and administrators in two-year colleges in West Texas. Based on these field tests, ambiguous questions were either rewritten or eliminated.

Sampling. Individual two-year institutions, rather than college districts or state systems, were used as the unit of analysis. Within each two-year institution, the vice-president of academic affairs, or a person in an equivalent position, was surveyed to obtain information about the college's minority faculty recruitment and retention programs. Given the major responsibility for faculty recruitment and retention that this administrator typically has, it was assumed that this individual would be knowledgeable both about the number of minority full-time faculty members employed at the college and about the college's minority faculty recruitment and retention programs.

The vice-president of academic affairs at each two-year college was identified by using either *Who's Who in Community, Technical, and Junior Colleges* (American Association of Community and Junior Colleges, 1991) or the *1993 HEP Higher Education Directory* (Higher Education Publications, 1993). These particular references were chosen because they are authoritative sources of recent information about administrative leaders at virtually every two-year college in the country. The recruitment questionnaire was sent to vice-presidents of academic affairs at all public two-year colleges identified from *Who's Who in Community, Technical, and Junior Colleges.* Of the 1,293 administrators sent the recruitment questionnaire in the spring of 1992, 701 responded after two waves, for an overall response rate of 54.2 percent. The retention questionnaire was sent to vice-presidents of academic affairs at all public and private not-for-profit two-year colleges identified from the 1993 *HEP Higher Education Directory.* Of 1,138 administrators sent the retention questionnaire in the spring of 1993, 686 responded after two waves, for an overall response rate of 60.3 percent.

Results and Discussion

Results of the surveys reveal both negative and positive predictors of a college's success in achieving faculty diversity.

Characteristics of the Sample. The vice-presidents of academic affairs who responded to the questionnaire tended to be white males, about 51 years of age, with either an Ed.D. or a Ph.D., and roughly 13 years of community college experience. Slightly more than one-quarter of the respondents were females, and slightly more than one-tenth were members of a minority group. This profile of respondents is quite similar to that revealed in an earlier study where 29.8 percent of two-year college administrators were female and 13.4 percent were minority (Hankin, 1984). In short, the respondents to this study had demographic backgrounds similar to community college administrators nationally.

Percentages of Minority Faculty. The percentage of minority faculty was calculated by dividing the number of faculty members of all colleges surveyed who belonged to the particular minority group by the number of full-time faculty members to be found within the total sample of colleges. Separate percentages were calculated for African American, American Indian, Mexican American, and Puerto Rican American faculty, as well as for the combination of these minority groups. A total of 61,089 full-time faculty were reported by the 701 institutions that responded to the recruitment questionnaire, which represents 69.2 percent of the 88,252 full-time faculty found in the two-year college sector (Astin, Korn, and Dey, 1991). A total of 61,840 full-time faculty were reported by the 686 institutions that responded to the retention questionnaire, which represents 70.1 percent of all full-time faculty found in the two-year sector. The percentages of underrepresented minority faculty found through the recruitment and retention questionnaires are compared in Table 5.1 with figures from the 1989–90 Higher Education Research Institute (HERI) Faculty Survey (Astin, Korn, and Dey, 1991) and the 1988 National Survey of Postsecondary Faculty (Russell, Fairweather, Hendrickson, and Zimbler, 1991). Results for individual racial/ethnic groups will be discussed using the data gathered from the 1993 retention questionnaire.

A total of 3,130 full-time African American faculty were reported by the respondents in this study, or 4.8 percent of all full-time faculty. This figure is higher than the percentage reported in either of the two recent national faculty studies. A total of 1,586 Mexican American faculty were reported, or 2.5 percent of all full-time faculty. This figure is higher than the percentage of Mexican American faculty reported in the 1989–1990 national study by Astin and colleagues. Similar data were not available from the National Center for Educational Statistics (NCES), because they reported aggregate data for Hispanics, rather than disaggregate data for Mexican Americans and Puerto Rican Americans. A total of 159 Puerto Rican American faculty were reported, or 0.3 percent of all full-time faculty, a figure slightly above the percentage reported in the study by Astin and others (1991). A total of 392 American Indian faculty were reported, or .6 percent of all full-time faculty, a percentage below that reported in the two national faculty studies.

Predicting the Percentage of Underrepresented Minority Faculty. The results of two regression analyses predicting the percentage of underrepresented minority faculty are displayed in Tables 5.2 and 5.3. The tables include the variables entered as significant predictors, along with simple correlations, standardized coefficients, and the F ratio.

Table 5.1. Percentage of Underrepresented Minority Full-Time Faculty at Two-Year Colleges

	Survey			
Minority Group	1992 Recruitment[a] Survey	1993 Retention[a] Survey	HERI[b] Survey	NCS[c] Survey
African American	4.9	4.8	4.0	3.0
American Indian	1.4	0.6	1.2	1.0
Mexican American	1.6	2.5	1.7	—
Puerto Rican American	0.3	0.3	0.2	—
Total	8.2	8.2	7.1	4.0

[a]Percentages were calculated by dividing the number of faculty members of all institutions surveyed who belonged to the particular minority group by the number of full-time faculty members to be found within the total sample of institutions.

[b]Percentages obtained from *The American College Teacher,* Astin, Korn, and Dey, 1991.

[c]Percentages obtained from *Profiles of Faculty in Higher Education Institutions, 1988,* Russell, Fairweather, Hendrickson, and Zimbler, 1991. Data are for public two-year colleges only.

Table 5.2. Prediction of the Percentage of
Underrepresented Minority Faculty (Recruitment Survey)

			Final Step		
Step	Variable	Zero r	Step Beta	Beta	F Ratio[a]
1	African American VP of academic affairs	.32	.32	.27	50.8
2	Contact with minority students	.31	.27	.11	46.0
3	Mexican American VP of academic affairs	.18	.18	.15	37.5
4	Contact with minority faculty	.29	.17	.09	32.2
5	Fitting in socially within the community	−.32	−.26	−.19	35.8
6	Amount of progress recruiting in the 1980s	.20	.12	.10	31.7
7	Minority faculty not available in arts/sciences	−.23	−.11	−.10	28.7
8	Interfering with faculty prerogatives	−.05	−.09	−.13	26.0
9	Minorities hired to staff ethnic-studies programs	.08	.09	.08	23.8
10	Minorities on board of trustees	.25	.15	.12	23.3
11	Recruiting minorities in private industry	.23	.09	.10	21.8
12	Canceling positions without minority applicant	.19	.09	.09	20.6

[a]F–Ratio greater than 1.76 significant at the .05 level. Mean = 8.3; S.D. = 12.1; Multiple R = .60; Adjusted R^2 = .34; Number of cases = 449.

Table 5.3. Prediction of the Percentage of
Underrepresented Minority Faculty (Retention Survey)

			Final Step		
Step	Variable	Zero r	Step Beta	Beta	F Ratio[a]
1	Contact with minority faculty	.31	.31	.18	46.3
2	African American VP of academic affairs	.30	.30	.28	49.7
3	American Indian VP of academic affairs	.20	.20	.15	41.7
4	Mexican American VP of academic affairs	.21	.17	.16	36.7
5	Fine arts department	.15	.14	.14	32.5
6	Contact with minority students	.30	.13	.10	28.8
7	Retaining faculty in the 1990s	.21	.13	.11	26.6
8	Absence of minority population in local community	−.22	−.10	−.09	24.3
9	Minorities on the board of trustees	.21	.11	.11	22.6

[a]F–Ratio greater than 1.89 significant at the .05 level. Mean = 7.9; S.D. = 11.3; Multiple R = .57; Adjusted R^2 = .31; Number of cases = 435.

Positive Predictors. These analyses revealed that having an African American, Mexican American, or American Indian vice-president of academic affairs is a positive predictor. Colleges with African American, Mexican American, or American Indian vice-presidents are more likely to have a high percentage of underrepresented minority faculty. Minority chief academic administrators may serve as strong advocates of the value of diversity on their college campuses. Such advocacy would be expected to lead to an increase in the institution's percentage of underrepresented minority faculty. The presence of minority chief academic administrators may also send a positive message to prospective minority faculty about the institution's commitment to diversity. Because of this perception, minority candidates may be more willing to apply for faculty positions at these institutions.

The amount of contact that vice-presidents of academic affairs have with both minority students and faculty are also positive predictors of the percentage of minority faculty—the greater the contact, the higher the percentage. These types of contact may serve to make the chief academic administrator more conscious of and sensitive to problems with the racial climate on campus, which would be expected to improve both the recruitment and retention of minority faculty.

Chief academic administrators with their highest degree in the fine arts is another positive predictor. Colleges whose vice-presidents of academic affairs have their highest degree in the fine arts are more likely to have a high percentage of underrepresented minority faculty. The reason for the positive influence of this particular disciplinary background is not immediately clear but deserves further attention in future research. Could it be that chief academic administrators with a fine arts background value the importance of diversity more than those from other academic or vocational backgrounds?

Having minorities serve on boards of trustees is also a positive predictor. Colleges that have minorities on their boards of trustees are more likely to have a high percentage of underrepresented minority faculty. Since members of two-year college boards of trustees are usually elected to office, colleges located in communities with a sizable minority population may be more likely to have minority board members than colleges located in communities with small minority populations. The racial composition of the community may make it easier for some colleges to take advantage of this recruitment and retention strategy than others. Minorities on college boards of trustees would be expected to be strong advocates of the value of diversity on their campuses.

Hiring minorities primarily to staff ethnic studies programs is another positive predictor. Colleges that hire minorities primarily to staff ethnic studies programs report a high percentage of underrepresented minority faculty. Two-year colleges located in communities with sizable minority populations may be more likely to have ethnic studies programs than other colleges as well as a high percentage of underrepresented minority faculty. Colleges with ethnic studies programs may also be more attractive job placements to minority candidates from outside the local community. Hiring minority faculty primarily for ethnic studies programs may also provide the chief academic administrator with a means to simultaneously increase the number of minority faculty, while maintaining "normative consensus and collegial relationships" in hiring decisions in other departments across campus (Exum, 1983, p. 390).

Recruiting minorities in private enterprise jobs to teach part time with the cooperation and support of their employer is another positive predictor. Colleges that utilize this strategy are more likely to have a high percentage of underrepresented minority faculty. Having minorities teach part time may make administrators and faculty more aware of qualified minority candidates when full-time positions become available. Such an awareness would be expected to lead to more minority faculty being hired. Minority faculty teaching part time may also be more likely to apply for full-time faculty positions when they become available. Any increase in the number of minority faculty applicants would be expected to lead to an increase in the number eventually hired.

Canceling positions where minority candidates have not been recruited into the applicant pool is the final positive predictor. Colleges that utilize this recruitment strategy are more likely to have a high percentage of underrepresented minority faculty. Departments that have canceled positions when minority candidates have not been recruited into the applicant pool may be motivated to disseminate information widely about faculty job openings to prospective candidates. Widespread dissemination of job openings would be expected to increase the number of minority applicants. This recruitment strategy may also serve as a symbol of the strength of the institution's commitment to diversity to prospective minority faculty. Such a demonstration of commitment would be expected to motivate more minority candidates to apply for faculty positions at these institutions.

Negative Predictors. Difficulty in having minority faculty fit in socially with the community is a negative predictor. The more strongly respondents agreed that minority faculty would have difficulty fitting in socially with their local community, the smaller was the college's percentage of underrepresented minority faculty. Chief academic administrators may be reluctant to recruit minority faculty because they anticipate difficulties with the minorities fitting in socially with their communities. Another possible reason for the negative influence is that minority faculty may avoid applying to colleges in communities where they themselves expect to have difficulty fitting in socially.

The unavailability of minority faculty for arts and science positions is another negative predictor. The more strongly respondents agreed that minority faculty are not available at their college for arts and science fields, the lower was their colleges' percentage of underrepresented minority faculty. Because of the limited number of minority students majoring in mathematics, science, and engineering-related fields, there may not be enough prospective minority faculty in some of these fields. Another possible reason for the negative influence is that chief academic officers who strongly agree with this statement may not actively recruit minority faculty because of their perception that few, if any, minority candidates are available. In short, this perception of unavailability may result in a self-fulfilling prophecy.

The absence of minorities in the local community is another negative predictor. The more strongly respondents agreed that the absence of a minority population in their local community is a common reason for minority faculty to leave their institution, the smaller was their college's percentage of underrepresented minority faculty. One possible reason for this negative influence is that communities without a minority population may not be able to offer minority faculty an adequate social support network. The absence of a social support network may result in higher minority faculty attrition rates for colleges located in such communities, and a lower subsequent percentage of underrepresented minority faculty.

Attempts to influence departments to hire minority faculty that evoke the red flag signaling interference with faculty prerogatives is another negative predictor. The more strongly respondents agreed that administrators should not interfere with faculty prerogatives, the lower was their college's percentage of underrepresented minority faculty. Academic administrators may choose to not actively recruit minority faculty in order to maintain "normative consensus and collegial relationships" in hiring decisions on campus (Exum, 1983, p. 390). This unwillingness to actively recruit minority candidates would be expected to result in a low percentage of minority faculty. Another possible negative influence is that minority candidates recruited by central administrators may be rejected by faculty as threats to their prerogatives. Faculty rejection of all minority candidates would also result in a low percentage of underrepresented minority faculty.

Policy Implications and Conclusions

In this study evidence is provided that African American, American Indian, Mexican American, and Puerto Rican American full-time faculty at two-year colleges are significantly underrepresented compared to the proportional representation of these minority groups in the U.S. population. Clearly, two-year college administrators need to address this issue of equity in their full-time faculty hiring and in tenure and promotion decisions.

Whether this underrepresentation is the result of attitudinal or structural factors cannot be determined with this study. Those who tend to ignore or discount the role of racism in higher education point to structural factors that impede progress in hiring and retaining minority faculty. A number of respondents indicated that structural factors such as the lack of minority candidates for faculty openings in many arts and science departments, as well as in occupational and technical departments, and the absence of a minority population in their local community are critical reasons for the underrepresentation of minority faculty at their college. Critics argue that these structural factors are simply rationalization for discrimination against minorities in full-time faculty hiring and tenure and promotion decisions. They argue that racist attitudes are the major reason that more progress has not been made in hiring and retaining minority full-time faculty (De la Luz Reyes and Halcon, 1988).

Policy implications vary depending on the emphasis one places on attitudinal versus structural factors. Those emphasizing structural barriers note that current economic constraints make it difficult to hire additional minority full-time faculty. Given the current economic situation facing many two-year colleges, individual colleges may have few resources to hire *any* full-time faculty. This structural problem probably needs to be addressed at the state, rather than at the local level. A state incentive program targeting additional funds for each minority full-time faculty hired at two-year colleges would provide the resources that two-year college administrators need to enhance their minority faculty recruitment programs.

One reason given for the possible structural barriers mentioned by a majority of respondents—the unavailability of minority faculty in arts and sciences, as well as occupational and technical fields—is the uneven distribution of academic majors among minority students that a number of researchers have noted (Astin, 1982; Blackwell, 1988; Garza, 1988). Minority students tend to avoid majors in mathematics and other science-related fields because they often lack the necessary high school math and science preparation. One possible solution to this lack of adequate preparation is for two-year college faculty and administrators to collaborate with elementary and secondary schools to increase minority student interest and preparation for these math and science-related fields. One type of collaboration might be for two-year colleges to sponsor science fairs or summer enrichment programs for elementary and secondary students focusing on science and math areas. Collaboration of two-year colleges with high schools in tech prep programs may also serve to increase the preparation of minority students in technical fields. It is clearly in the best interest of two-year colleges to collaborate with elementary and secondary schools in trying to attract and prepare minority students for faculty positions in mathematics, science, and technology-related areas at their colleges.

A third structural barrier mentioned by a majority of the respondents was that prospective minority faculty prefer employment in business and industry to employment in two-year colleges. A number of researchers have noted that academic salaries rank far below salaries in business and industry (Bowen and Schuster, 1986; Bunzel, 1990). Two-year college administrators may be able to compete with business and industry for minority candidates by stressing the intrinsic satisfaction and greater prestige typically involved in a two-year college academic career. Minorities from private enterprise might also be recruited to teach part time with the support of their employers in order to make them more aware of the intrinsic satisfaction of a two-year college career.

Those emphasizing structural factors also point to the absence of a minority population in the local community as a major barrier to retaining minority faculty. The lack of a social support network in the community may make it difficult to keep minority faculty at one's college. One possible solution is for the college to take a proactive role in providing opportunities to integrate minority faculty into the social networks. Activities that serve to integrate minority faculty socially into the college community may serve to compensate for their relative lack of social integration within the larger community.

Those emphasizing attitudinal factors underscore that eliminating these structural barriers may be a necessary but not a sufficient condition to significantly improve the number of minority full-time faculty. Removing structural barriers will not change racist attitudes which may be preventing the hiring and retention of minority faculty on some campuses. Those who emphasize attitudinal factors as the main barrier to minority faculty recruitment and retention point to the need to hire minorities for highly visible leadership positions. In this study it was found that having minorities serve on the board of trustees or as vice-presidents of academic affairs have strong positive influences on a college's percentage of underrepresented minority full-time faculty. Representatives of many two-year colleges may argue that they already have an administrator, often a minority, responsible for affirmative action. Slightly under one-half of the respondents reported that they had such an affirmative action officer. Having such an officer responsible for affirmative action, however, was found not to be significantly related to the college's percentage of minority faculty. This finding underscores the importance of hiring minorities for highly visible leadership positions. Such minority leaders can serve both as advocates for diversity in faculty hiring and as counterweights to any racist tendencies which might exist on college campuses.

Those who emphasize attitudinal barriers are also extremely critical of hiring practices which relegate minority faculty primarily or exclusively to ethnic studies departments (Garza, 1988; De la Luz Reyes and Halcon, 1988). This study revealed that this practice has a positive influence on the percentage of underrepresented minority faculty. One consequence of this practice, however, is that minority full-time faculty may not be considered for vacancies in other arts and sciences or in occupational and technical fields. Arce (1978) and Olivas (1986) argue that this practice of specialized minority hiring for minority slots "is a more formal co-optation of Hispanic concerns . . . which relieves the institution of the need to integrate throughout their ranks" (Olivas, 1986, p. 14). Although this practice does lead to some increases in the representation of minority faculty, it places an artificial ceiling on the number of minority faculty that might be hired throughout the institution. Clearly, this practice needs to be substituted with one that encourages the recruitment and hiring of minority faculty in *all* departments.

Those who emphasize attitudinal barriers also believe that faculty positions should be canceled when no minority candidates have been recruited into the candidate pool. In this study it was found that colleges that use this strategy tend to have high percentages of minority faculty. By forcing colleges to conduct a widespread, thorough search for minority candidates, this practice may serve as an additional counterweight to racist tendencies which may exist at some two-year colleges. That less than 15 percent of respondents reported using this particular recruitment strategy is interesting to these authors. One might expect that chief academic administrators would be reluctant to use this strategy, given that it often evokes the red flag of interference with their prerogatives among faculty. Despite potential opposition from faculty, this recruitment strategy is a particularly effective means of increasing the number of underrepresented minority full-time faculty. Many two-year college administrators would be well-advised to consider using this strategy in addressing the issue of equity in faculty hiring.

In conclusion, both attitudinal and structural barriers need to be removed before improvements can be made in the percentage of minority full-time faculty at two-year colleges. Addressing structural barriers is a necessary but not sufficient condition for improving faculty diversity. If two-year colleges are to fulfill their mission of providing equity and excellence by significantly increasing the numbers of underrepresented minority full-time faculty, efforts need to be redoubled to remove both structural and attitudinal barriers.

References

American Association of Community and Junior Colleges. *Who's Who in Community, Technical, and Junior Colleges, 1991.* Washington, D.C.: American Association of Community and Junior Colleges, 1991.

Arce, C. "Chicano Participation in Academia: A Case of Academic Colonialism." *Grito del Sol: A Chicano Quarterly,* 1978, *3,* 75–104.

Astin, A. W. *Minorities in American Higher Education.* San Francisco: Jossey-Bass, 1982.

Astin, A. W., Korn, W. S., and Dey, E. L. *The American College Teacher.* Los Angeles: Higher Education Research Institute, 1991.

Banks, W. M. "Afro-American Scholar in the University." *American Behavioral Scientist,* 1984, *27* (3), 325–338.

Blackwell, J. E. "Faculty Issues: The Impact on Minorities." *Review of Higher Education,* 1988, *11* (4), 417–434.

Bowen, H. R., and Schuster, J. H. *American Professors.* Oxford: Oxford University Press, 1986.

Bunzel, J. H. "Faculty Hiring: Problems and Practices." *American Scholar,* 1990, *59* (1), 39–52.

De la Luz Reyes, M., and Halcon, J. J. "Racism in Academia: The Old Wolf Revisited." *Harvard Educational Review,* 1988, *58* (3), 299–314.

Exum, W. H. "Climbing the Crystal Stair: Values, Affirmative Action, and Minority Faculty." *Social Problems,* 1983, *30* (4), 383–399.

Exum, W. H., Menges, R. J., Watkins, B., and Berglund, P. "Making It at the Top." *American Behavioral Scientist,* 1984, *27* (3), 301–324.

Garza, H. "The 'Barrioization' of Hispanic Faculty." *Educational Record,* 1988, *68* (4), 122–124.

Hankin, J. N. "Where the (Affirmative) Action Is: The Status of Minorities and Women Among the Faculty and Administrators of Public Two-Year Colleges." *Journal of College and University Personnel Association,* 1984, *35* (4), 36–39.

Higher Education Publications. *HEP Higher Education Directory.* Falls Church, Va.: Higher Education Publications, 1993.

Linthicum, D. S. *The Dry Pipeline: Increasing the Flow of Minority Faculty.* Washington, D.C.: National Council of State Directors of Community and Junior Colleges, 1989.

Menges, R. J., and Exum, W. H. "Barriers to the Progress of Women and Minority Faculty." *Journal of Higher Education,* 1983, *54* (2), 123–144.

Mickelson, R. A., and Oliver, M. L. "The Demographic Fallacy of the Black Academic: Does Quality Rise to the Top?" In W. R. Allen, E. G. Epps, and N. Z. Haniff (eds.), *College in Black and White*. Albany: State University of New York Press, 1991.

Moore, W. "Black Faculty in White Colleges: A Dream Deferred." *Educational Record*, 1988, 68 (4), 116–121.

Olivas, M. A. "Research on Latino College Students: A Theoretical Framework and Inquiry." In M. A. Olivas (ed.), *Latino College Students*. New York: Teachers College Press, 1986.

Reed, R. J. "Affirmative Action in Higher Education: Is It Necessary?" *Journal of Negro Education*, 1983, 52 (3), 332–349.

Reed, R. J. "Faculty Diversity: An Educational and Moral Imperative in Search of Institutional Commitment." *Journal of Educational Equity and Leadership*, 1986, 6 (4), 274–294.

Russell, S. H., Fairweather, J. S., Hendrickson, R. M., and Zimbler, L. J. *Profiles of Faculty in Higher Education Institutions*. Washington, D.C.: National Center for Education Statistics, 1991.

Smelser, N. J., and Content, R. *The Changing Academic Market*. Berkeley: University of California Press, 1980.

U.S. Department of Commerce, Bureau of Census. *1990 Census Profile: Race and Hispanic Origin, Number 2*. Washington, D.C.: U.S. Government Printing Office, 1991.

U.S. Department of Education. *Trends in Racial/Ethnic Enrollment in Higher Education: Fall 1980 Through Fall 1990*. Washington, D.C.: Government Printing Office, 1992.

U.S. Equal Employment Opportunity Commission. *Higher Education Staff Information Report*. Washington, D.C.: Government Printing Office, 1990.

RONALD D. OPP is assistant professor in the Higher Education Program, Texas Tech University, Lubbock.

ALBERT B. SMITH is professor and coordinator in the Higher Education Program, Texas Tech University, Lubbock.

Community colleges are changing in the missions they perform and the constituencies they serve, and it is imperative that the faculty reflect these changes.

Bridging the Gap: Recruitment and Retention of Minority Faculty Members

Jerry Sue Owens, Frank W. Reis, Kathryn M. Hall

Educating multi-ethnic students for life in a multicultural world is one of the greatest challenges facing institutions of higher learning in the 1990s. Community colleges can be justly proud of their tradition as "open door institutions." They strive for both excellence and equity in providing opportunity for students to access higher education. In this decade of diversity, it would be wonderful if these colleges could be equally proud of equity in their faculties. While student populations have grown more diverse, the faculty ranks have remained racially and ethnically static.

Forty-five percent of all minorities in higher education are enrolled in community colleges. In Fall 1990, ethnic minorities comprised 23 percent of all students enrolled at community colleges. African Americans are the largest group, making up 45 percent of total minorities enrolled. Hispanics were 35 percent, Asian/Pacific Islanders 18 percent, and American Indians 5 percent (Pluta, 1991; Shantz, 1992). By August 1991 minority student enrollment had increased to 30 percent (Triplett, 1991).

California, the state with the largest number of community colleges, provides the best example of the large proportion of minority students enrolled in these institutions. According to Lisa Lapin (1993), the state's 107 community colleges currently enroll 1.5 million Californians, one-third of whom are from minority groups.

The 176,000 Latino students at California's two-year campuses were more than triple the Latino enrollment at all University of California and California State University campuses combined. Likewise, in New York more than half the City University of New York (CUNY) system consists of minority students.

Bronx Community College, as reported by Dr. Roscoe C. Brown, Jr., its president, has a student population that is 48 percent African American, 45 percent Hispanic, 4 percent white, and 3 percent Asian. These figures are proof of dedication to fairness in minority access to community colleges, but what is the mix of faculty charged with educating these diverse students?

According to Astin, Korn, and Dey (1991), the full-time minority faculty represent approximately 10 percent of the teaching force in community colleges. While the classrooms, laboratories, libraries, gyms, and cafeterias are replete with numerous "faces of color," the faculty does not reflect this diversity.

Benefits of Minority Faculty

One of the most effective and most visible support systems for students is faculty with whom they can identify and receive strength. Richardson and Bender (1987) eloquently state the benefits of minority faculty on minority students: "The single most effective strategy for producing changes in faculty attitudes toward minority students may well be the recruitment of minority faculty members. In a meeting between faculty members, the tone of a discussion was altered by the arrival of a black faculty member. Not only did she offer important insights into the needs of minority students, but her very presence elicited sensitivity to the issues of working with minority students from the non-minority colleagues" (p. 69). Minority faculty who come from backgrounds similar to their students bring a special sensitivity that suggests a mutual understanding of cultural differences. It is beneficial for minority students to see members of their race and ethnicity in prominent faculty positions because reflections of one's self are vital affirmations of worth and value.

Likewise, it is equally important for majority students to be exposed to minority faculty. Students of all races are entitled to the benefits of a multiracial, multicultural teaching force whose members serve ably as role models and mentors.

Seymour Fersh (1974), professor in the Social/Behavioral/Humanities Department at Brevard Community College (Florida), observed that ignorance about others perpetuates ignorance about ourselves because it is only through comparisons that we can discover personal differences and similarities. "The glass through which we view other cultures/races serves not only as a window but also as a mirror in which we can see a reflection of our own way of life" (p. 31). Thus, the holistic college experience requires diversity throughout the institutional family.

Context of Minority Participation in the Community College

Recruitment and retention of minority faculty is essential. Madeleine Green (1989) exquisitely summarizes the need: "A diverse faculty is essential to a pluralistic campus. Faculty create the curriculum and determine the quality of the experience in every classroom. They serve as teachers, mentors, advisors and role models. In a word, faculty are the core of the institution. Without the contributions of minority individuals, no faculty or institution can be complete" (p. 81). Such diversification is not a simple task; rather it is a multiple process that must integrate and involve all individuals and elements within the college community. While certain strategies are useful in attracting and retaining desirable candidates, the best one is the creation of a quality college environment that reflects attributes attractive to everyone. Minority candidates are looking for what every other candidate desires: respect, warmth, genuineness, fairness, and support.

In addition, it is important to understand the extraordinary demands that create tensions for minority faculty: large time allocations counseling minority students, service as a role model, considerable committee demands as the minority "resident expert," and finally, visible and active community service. All minority faculty members confront tensions in the balancing act between the expectations and demands of the college, students, and the community (Mitchell, 1983; Green, 1989). If the college sincerely intends to make a commitment to minority faculty, then the college must recognize the special demands that faculty will face—and these issues must be addressed constructively. Without this approach, recruitment and retention cannot be accomplished.

Given the special strengths of community colleges in individualizing instruction and structuring student success, they must bring equal effort to individualizing and structuring programs for all faculty.

Recruitment of Minority Faculty: The First Step

If diversifying the college calls for a major restructuring and change in attitude, this process must have that commitment at the highest levels: the president and board of trustees. This dedication must be not only verbal but also visceral and unabating. Parnell (1990) characterizes mission clarification and definition of institutional values as the priority task of the college president and goes on to state: "Most individuals are value driven, and they can be motivated to live up to institutional values if these are clearly communicated by both the practice and preaching of the college president" (p. 26). Such authority emanates from respect for position, desire for direction, and control of rewards.

For diversification to succeed, the president and the board must be willing to express this concept as part of the official institutional vision and be ready to stake their authority and allocate power on such commitment throughout the entire college process. The board and president must set the mission and agenda, and then work with the rest of the college to set realistic goals.

As important as it is to have total and unwavering commitment at the top, it is just as important to have this commitment accepted at all levels. While the president can do much to have his or her views accepted as official within the institution, it is not until the overall plan is developed and accepted that it can be implemented as policy.

Again, this is a "major restructuring and change in outlook," and as such, only a unified commitment can result in a unified program. Strategies that can successfully elicit this commitment are similar to those used for implementing institution-wide programs such as total quality management or effective schooling. Everyone must see how the new vision will benefit the college totally, and even more, how it will benefit them as individuals. The college family must understand that diversification will enhance the institution through enrollment growth, greater fund availability, increased support services, more institutional prestige, and favorable publicity. Working for a college that is highly respected and a quality institution can contribute a great deal to self-image.

Minority Faculty Recruitment: Knowing Where to Look

Broadening the recruitment base involves learning to look at relevant, new opportunities. Graduate school programs provide one source of potential faculty for community colleges. While many of these programs focus on development of administrators, some graduate students seek to impart their leadership in the classroom. Arizona State University (Richard C. Richardson), University of Michigan (Richard Alfred), University of California at Los Angeles (Arthur Cohen), North Carolina State University (George Baker and George Vaughan), University of Texas (John Roueche), and George Mason University in Virginia (Gustavo Mellander) have education departments with an emphasis on community college leadership and teaching that provide a source for minority faculty recruitment.

According to the July 1993 *Black Issues in Higher Education,* 60 percent of the current class in the University of Texas at Austin's Community College Leadership Program (CCLP) are minorities and women. Gustavo Mellander, senior scholar in Community College Education at George Mason University in Virginia, sees "a window of opportunity for minority faculty especially to replace the high number of retiring community college professors—approximately 60 percent by the year 2000" (Rodriguez, 1993, p. 45). Thus, its doctor of arts in community college education is designed to educate future college professors. One of the most vital sources for obtaining minority faculty remains "growing your own." As colleges look internally for prospective faculty, the population of students, alumni, clerical staff, and advisory board members are likely candidates for teacher training and graduate programs. No one should be overlooked, since some may currently possess the appropriate required credentials for classroom instruction. It is not unusual to discover that secretaries and lab and administrative assistants have graduate degrees in a specific discipline. Recruitment of these individuals into teaching via career change is often a matter of presenting the opportunity and providing some initial orientation and teaching methodology preparation.

Community college students also represent an untapped source for future minority teachers. Triplett (1991) indicates that while only 13 percent of the bachelor's degrees conferred in 1987 were awarded to minorities, nearly one-fourth of the students enrolled in community colleges belonged to a minority group. A recent study revealed that nearly 50 percent of the teachers who received their teacher training at Florida's public universities first attended a Florida community college.

Collaborative efforts between universities (particularly departments of education) and community college faculty and administrators could enhance transfer and teacher training for minority students. Students whose lower division experience occurred at a community college may experience a sense of familiarity and commitment to this area of higher education. They know best the value of education; they have already defied the odds and perhaps see teaching in the community college environment as a way to "give something back."

Other internal sources of minority teacher recruitment may be the administrative ranks, student development/services, and continuing education. Often individuals with teaching credentials and skills who want to affiliate with community colleges enter these institutions through the first available position. Encouraging college professionals to consider teaching options could prove beneficial to the goal of increasing minority faculty. Some colleges promote part-time teaching for these employees as initial transitional steps to full-time faculty positions.

External recruitment activities can focus on minority media (newspapers, radio stations, and journals). Many of these sources are closely aligned to the culture of a particular minority community, especially where language is an important factor such as it is with Hispanics. Community centers, church announcements, bulletins, and bulletin boards provide an additional means for outreach and notification of available positions. Personal communications via community leaders can serve as information networks to alert interested individuals to job openings in teaching.

One final innovative approach to finding qualified candidates as alternative recruitment sources are business, industry, and military partnerships. Individuals in these partnerships have strong credentials, often including advanced degrees. Many will welcome an opportunity to consider transferring into college faculty positions. Still others would like to have the option of teaching on a part-time basis. Given the strength of some college-industry partnerships, personnel might even be made available to community colleges as loaned executives in an attractive financial arrangement.

Recruitment of Minority Faculty: Keeping an Open Mind

In evaluating the credentials of candidates, search committees should be open to alternative strategies for assessing a candidate's overall experience. It is quite possible for an applicant to possess the same degree of proficiency through a broad range of non-traditional experiences.

Making sure that the search committee includes diversity in ethnicity and background is another way to broaden the range of options examined and to ensure their sensitivity to alternative approaches. If there are not enough individuals in the college department to serve on the committee, a successful strategy practiced on many campuses is to include minority professionals from the nearby community (Duran, 1993).

Retention of Minority Faculty: Follow-Through

Once a minority faculty member has accepted an offer of employment, the college focus should immediately shift to retention. Given all the effort involved in actively recruiting good minority candidates, it is essential that resources be devoted to a plan that enables retention. This plan must be based on a clear understanding of the problems minority faculty face.

Minority faculty at predominantly majority community colleges often feel marginalized or even invisible. Gappa and Leslie, in their book *The Invisible Faculty* (1993), discuss the status and integration of adjunct faculty at institutions of higher education. Parallels can be drawn between part-time and minority faculty who remain on the periphery of the institution. Conscious efforts must be made by deans, department chairs, and division heads to incorporate all faculty into the decision-making process of the college, to mainstream the teaching assignments and include them in all facets of campus life and activities.

This requires a supportive environment of collegiality. Such a community is based on cooperative fellowship, working together in harmony and respect toward commonly shared goals that offer open access to higher education and create opportunities for success. It will stimulate members to grow, develop, and maximize potential; it will expose participants to a world of new ideas and experiences; it will provide a comfort level of support that encourages risk taking; and it will create empowerment through participation in decision making.

To encourage minority retention, for example, community colleges should schedule activities that require all teaching faculty to interact on a regular basis. All faculty should be required to participate in diversity training. Staff development programs in areas such as teaching skills, cross-cultural communication, at-risk learning, personal computers, and research skills can also help solidify staff relationships.

Formal mechanisms that will help new members feel included can feature such items as campus tours for faculty and their spouses; information packets (including information on the adjoining community as well); and assistance with college and campus resources, housing, shopping, and community services. There should be a required orientation for all new staff. Inviting participation in formal and informal activities will signal to new members that they are indeed part of the college family. Social and professional interactions are crucial to a sense of acceptance.

Conclusion

Community colleges are changing radically in the missions they perform and the constituencies they serve. It is extremely important that their very core, their faculty, reflect these changes. This is particularly vital to the strength of the institutions and to the students they serve. Given the fact that students of color make up over 30 percent of the total number of community college students, the minority faculty percentage must be increased over its current ten percent level.

Successful minority faculty recruitment and retention programs must be founded on college-wide goals and commitment. They share strategies that will lead to successful minority recruitment resulting in increased and successful minority retention. Both depend on an environment based on inclusion, caring, and respect. Everyone should feel that the program is not only legitimate, but also a benefit to the institution and themselves. There must be strong support from the president and the board, and there must also be shared consensus from the rest of the community. "Building community must, of course, begin at home. If the college itself is not held together by a larger vision, if trustees, administrators, faculty, and students are not inspired by purposes that go beyond credits and credentials, the community college will be unable to build effective networks of collaboration beyond the campus. If the college itself is not a model community, it cannot advocate community to others" (Commission on The Future of Community Colleges, *Building Communities: A Vision for a New Century*).

References

Astin, N. W., Korn, W. S., and Dey, E. L. *National Norms for 1989–90 HERI Faculty Survey*. Los Angeles: Higher Education Research Institute, UCLA, 1991.

Commission on the Future of Community College. *Building Communities: A Vision for a New Century*. Washington, D.C.: American Association of Community and Junior Colleges, 1988.

Duran, R. In De Anza College Television in Association with the Community College Satellite Network, *Hispanic Issues in Higher Education: The Politics, Prerequisites, and Presumptions*. May 5, 1993. Stanford, Calif.: Stanford University Press.

Fersh, S. (ed.). *Learning About Peoples and Cultures*. Evanston, Ill.: McDougal, Littell, and Company, 1974.

Gappa, J. M., and Leslie, D. W. *The Invisible Faculty*. San Francisco: Jossey-Bass, 1993.

Green, M. F. (ed). *Minorities on Campus: A Handbook for Enhancing Diversity*. Washington, D.C.: American Council on Education, 1989.

Lapin, L. "Minorities Hardest Hit by 300 Percent Fee Hike at California Community Colleges, Say Educators." *Black Issues in Higher Education*, 1993, 9, 25.

Mitchell, J. "Visible, Vulnerable and Viable: Emerging Perspectives of a Minority Professor." In J. H. Cones III, J. F. Noonan, and D. Janha (eds.), *Teaching Minority Students*. New Directions for Teaching and Learning, no. 16. San Francisco: Jossey-Bass, 1983.

Parnell, D. *Dateline 2000: The New Higher Education Agenda*. Washington, D.C.: Community College Press, 1990.

Pluta, M. J. *National Higher Education Statistics, Fall 1991 Early Estimates,* Report No. 92–032. Washington, D.C.: National Center for Education Statistics, 1991.

Richardson, R. C., and Bender, L. W. *Fostering Minority Access and Achievement in Higher Education.* San Francisco: Jossey-Bass, 1987.

Rodriguez, R. "University of Texas at Austin Leads Way with Its Community College Graduate Program." *Black Issues In Higher Education,* 1993, *10* (10), 43–46.

Shantz, N. B. "Trends in Racial/Ethnic Enrollment in Higher Education." *U.S. Education,* 1992.

Triplett, J. R. "The Nation's Community Colleges Are an Untapped Resource for New Minority Teachers." *Black Issues in Higher Education,* 1991, *8,* 88.

JERRY SUE OWENS is president of Cuyahoga Community College in Cleveland, Ohio.

FRANK W. REIS is executive vice-president of Cuyahoga Community College in Cleveland, Ohio.

KATHRYN M. HALL is director of diversity at Cuyahoga Community College in Cleveland, Ohio.

An educated populace, including an educated minority population, is essential to the economic and social well-being of the nation.

Recruitment and Retention of Minority Faculty

Piedad F. Robertson, Ted Frier

It is a powerful image: the slow, steady pan of the camera as the picture of young African American faces come into view, their eyes hopeful, focused on a crossroad, asking for our help. Then the message: "A mind is a terrible thing to waste."

This advertising slogan from the United Negro College Fund has become as much a part of the national landscape as the nationwide effort to increase the number of minorities graduating from our colleges and universities. So much attention has been devoted in recent years to promoting diversity in higher education not because we are soft-hearted, but because we are hard-headed; not because we harbor a sentimental disposition to do "something" for those who have been historically disadvantaged, but because we have made a realistic appraisal of the opportunities that will be lost to the nation if we do not bring the ever-growing minority population into the higher education community, both as students and as faculty.

This transformation in emphasis lies along the fault of converging economic and demographic trends. By the year 2000 it is estimated that 75 percent of all workers will be in jobs requiring mental, rather than physical, exertion (*Workforce 2000, Executive Summary,* 1991). The greatest growth will be for workers in professional and technical occupations such as management, information processing, health care, and law. In Massachusetts alone, state labor force studies estimate that 80 percent of the new jobs will require postsecondary education and 33 percent will require four years of college. By contrast, just eight years ago 22 percent of all jobs in the state required a bachelor's degree.

To be competitive in the new global market, workers will need more higher order skills than they currently possess. These new workers will require

 65

problem-identifying skills in order to understand current and future needs. They will need problem-solving skills in order to put things together in new ways. They will have to be creative thinkers, able to respond quickly to changing technologies. Guaranteeing each individual an equal opportunity to achieve his or her full potential must be the first priority of any just society. A complicated society needs men and women who are competent to comprehend these issues, who understand the past so that they can embrace the future free from the suffocating fear that ignorance breeds, and who are capable of making wise decisions for themselves, their families, and their society. All of these ambitions are impossible to achieve without access to education.

At the same time that dramatic changes are occurring in the character of the workplace, a significant revolution is taking place in the composition of the work force. By the year 2000, immigrants and minorities will be the mainstay of the work force. Almost half will be women. Minorities will hold almost one position in every five. New immigrants will constitute a like number. The traditional white male work force will account for only 15 percent of the total by the year 2000—a startling decline from the 47 percent of the labor force who were white males in 1985 (*Workforce 2000, Executive Summary,* 1991).

The national challenge for the foreseeable future is to devise ways to improve upon the modest educational gains among minorities at precisely the time when the demand for an educated minority work force is accelerating.

Now, the entire discussion of diversity has become as badly garbled in higher education as it has in other settings. As an issue of "right" or "fairness" or "justice," the dialogue on expanding minority representation on college campuses immediately leads to impasse. The legitimate claim that teaching and administrative personnel in higher education institutions should reflect the composition of the communities they serve can be balanced with an equally valid assertion: Individuals should be treated as individuals, not as demographic statistics. Only in the context of the unique contributions that minority faculty and staff can make to improve the education of minorities can the case be made for affirmative action. If minority students are to succeed, it is important that schools cultivate a welcoming atmosphere. Part of the texture of such an atmosphere is having minority role models among the faculty. The primary reason we are interested in minority faculty is because they establish in the minds of the community and the student that there is a commitment to diversity. Additionally, they serve as networks for minority students and assist institutions committed to diversity by recruiting minority students themselves.

To understand why minority faculty possess certain unique "job qualifications," it is necessary to understand the ingredients that contribute to the success or failure of minority students. Some are obvious. The quality of schools the students attended and how well they did are major factors. Straight-A students are 25 times more likely to complete college in four years than C students are. Family incomes are important—not only as a source of tuition costs, but also as a buffer against the pressures high school students face to immediately get a job. The educational level of the parents is critical, for 60 percent of students come from families where the parents did not graduate from high school (Education Commission of the States and the State Higher Education Executive Officers, 1987).

Other factors are more subtle. Whether minority students succeed or fail in college is determined as much by the attitudes they bring to education as by the education aptitudes they possess. Foremost is the belief in the value of higher education, not only that of the students, but also of their peers, relatives, and familiar community. Without adult mentors who can show these students the tangible value of higher education, or explain what the college experience is all about, many minority students, even promising students, may believe that continued schooling is incompatible with attaining adulthood. "Incognegroes" is the expressive phrase that Harvard professor Glenn Loury has invented to describe African American students at prestigious universities who conceal their educational achievement from acquaintances in their home communities (Education Commission of the States and the State Higher Education Executive Officers, 1987).

Clearly, what minority faculty contribute is their ability to serve as role models for minority students who may have gone through life without a single close acquaintance who graduated from college. Minority faculty are also visible reminders that a student is attending an institution committed to diversity. Institutions committed to minority success are fundamentally different in character from those that give a perfunctory nod to this achievement. It is a difference between an institution willing to accommodate minority students, and one which makes the success of minority students an important factor in its own calculation of whether the institution is succeeding or failing.

Richardson (1989) has identified three phases in the evolution of an institution from one indifferent to minorities to one that is supportive. In the first stage, institutions simply erase barriers to participation. This can be done through flexible admission practices, financial aid, transition programs, and outreach to public schools. In the second stage, colleges and universities improve the campus climate and provide learning assistance to students who lack adequate preparation. They also recruit a diverse faculty and administration and thereby provide advocates and role models for the new student populations.

Helping students adjust to the rigors of the college experience will help retention, but will not improve graduation rates unless there is an accompanying change in teaching and learning practices, which occurs in the third stage. For this to occur, faculty must become involved in helping more diversely prepared students achieve academic success in all majors. This involves more sophisticated student assessments that take into account minority students' unique backgrounds and circumstances, learning assistance programs, and a commitment to success through improved teaching. Teachers must change their approach to teaching. They must incorporate different teaching styles in order to accommodate the learning styles of minority students. Teachers must be flexible to avoid insisting that their students learn the way they learned. Minority students do bring different learning styles and backgrounds to the classroom, and a teacher should acknowledge that by creating a hospitable learning environment and incorporating respect for other cultures into their courses. When the faculty are actively involved in minority success, they can create the necessary climate that sends a message to minority students that they can do it. Students know when they are in the company of individuals or institutions that really want to help, and this is reinforced by a visible minority presence among an institution's faculty and staff (Richardson, Matthews, and Finney, 1992).

Recruiting Minority Faculty

Any effort to improve the campus environment for minority students by expanding the number of minority staff and faculty role models ultimately collides with a harsh reality. Despite decades of hiring goals set by individual departments, colleges, and universities, despite the promises to do a better job diversifying the faculty, despite all memorandums of understanding or letters of agreement, minorities still account for only a slender sliver of college faculties nationwide. The latest federal data show that in four-year colleges and universities during the academic years 1991 to 1992, about 12.3 percent of the nation's full-time professor corps were African American, Hispanic, Indian, or Asian. This figure represents only a slight increase from two years before when 11.5 percent of the teaching corps was minority and represents relatively flat gains throughout the past decade (Magner, 1993).

Inevitably, the fates of minority students and minority faculty are inextricably intertwined. We cannot do a better job of graduating minority students unless the minority faculty representation is larger, and we cannot augment that representation unless more minorities pass through the nation's graduate programs. This dilemma might be what policy wonks refer to as a "structural deficit." Neither is it of much help that higher education institutions across the country have been mired in a period of budgetary retrenchment over the last five years, making it difficult to free up new positions that might be filled by minority academics.

The shallow pool of potential minority candidates for faculty positions is a very real difficulty. And it is unlikely to improve anytime soon. The Educational Testing Service recently reported significant shifts in minority career paths. More minority students than ever before are now majoring in engineering, business, health, and biology at the undergraduate level. Fewer are going into education, the social sciences, or other undergraduate fields that are typical avenues to graduate school study. As the ETS reported, between 1976 and 1989 the number of degrees in education granted to minority students declined by 56 percent. There was a 9 percent decline in the social sciences. Meanwhile, minority graduates of engineering programs increased 290 percent, business 118 percent, health professions 58 percent, and biological and life sciences 38 percent (Educational Testing Service, 1992).

Now, we should be careful not to shout "crisis" too soon. While it might be inconvenient for deans and department heads looking to improve minority representation on their faculties, there is nothing particularly sinister in this shift toward degrees that lead directly to employment upon graduation. It may be nothing more than a transitory stage, the first step in the natural and healthy process by which underrepresented communities establish themselves among the ranks of the professional middle class. We know from experience that it is far more likely that the sons and daughters of financially secure professionals will pursue, say, a doctorate in the humanities, than it is for the first member of a family attending college to do so.

These trends should be seen as challenges to overcome, not excuses for inaction. And some institutions have been better than others at meeting these challenges. Some institutions exacerbate the supply problem by accepting only those applicants who have attended prestigious universities. Other two- and four-year institutions mimic this behavior when they close doors by insisting on rigid qualifications for their applicants for faculty and staff positions by requiring a certain specified period of service in a narrow range of occupations.

This exclusionary practice is as bad as admitting only those students who scored within a particular percentile on the SAT, when a far better approach would be to define the talents a job requires and then spend time assessing whether a particular candidate possesses those talents. Imaginative college administrators can create opportunities for minority faculty and staff where none existed before. They can open doors, facilitate contacts, create cushions against failure, and provide opportunities for success. But all of this demands the courage on the part of administrators and institutions to take risks. No one will ever lose money betting on the heavy favorites to show, but the big pay-offs come to those who make their wager on the long shots.

Faced with a shortage of candidates, some institutions do more than sit back and complain. More two- and four-year institutions should follow the example of those who actively cultivate future faculty from the undergraduate level on. Duke, for instance, has adopted a "grow your own" approach. Once advertising for a new physics professor, Duke received only six applications from African Americans out of several hundred submitted. This prompted department administrators to take matters into its own hands. "Had we not raised him ourselves," said physics department chairman Lawrence Evans of a new faculty member, "we'd probably have no black faculty now." Jacqueline Looney, assistant dean for graduate recruitment, said what makes the differences is that "faculty members in the department are truly committed to not only recruiting these students, but retaining them and graduating them."

Like minority students, minority faculty members become victims of revolving doors unless things are put in place at an institution to nourish them. Once recruited, institutions should do more for their minority faculty than simply putting them in the classroom and congratulating themselves. These faculty have the potential to be active role models for students, the best advertising an institution can have in attracting students from the minority community. But the added burdens this places on young academics should be recognized by institutions, especially in promotion and tenure decisions. Hired in part because of the unique contributions they can make to an institution as members of a minority group, these faculty members will become early casualties unless they are welcomed and valued members of the campus community.

One young black professor in Maryland summed it up well: Most institutions, except the historically black institutions, hire blacks in token numbers. Therefore, typically when black persons are hired for faculty positions, they are role models, advisors, counselors, advocates, and sympathetic listeners for black students. As a result, they are often drawn into activities unrelated to their competencies or interests. Minority faculty often feel that they must respond to the needs of minority students who frequently experience alienation in predominantly white institutions. The dilemma is to work hard and meet the traditional requirements for tenure while responding directly to student demands and departmental and institutional expectations to not only work with minority students but be the "minority representative" on every committee (*Access Is Not Enough,* 1989).

Like ensuring student success, the frustrations of minority faculty, such as those above, are the sorts of issues that are addressed in more positive and meaningful ways once minority representation reaches a critical mass at an institution.

More than most other higher education institutions, community colleges seem to be in a better position to recruit and retain minority faculty, for a number of reasons. There is already a heavier minority representation on campus, contributing to an inviting environment. Additionally, community colleges are less vulnerable to the shortage of minority doctoral candidates graduating each year. Because their curriculums are more directly tied to the professions into which minority graduates seem to be going, community colleges have a larger pool from which to draw.

Further, a successful effort to recruit more minorities into teaching ranks demands more than simply buying display advertisements in higher education publications. It demands seeking out potential candidates where they live and work. This is fully consonant with the community college's mission of direct involvement in its local city or region. Some community colleges have been wonderfully inventive in opening their doors to minority faculty. Some meet regularly with civic organizations, churches, and businesses. Some colleges make sure to advertise in minority publications. They promote the college in the minority community and keep groups posted about potential and real job openings. Others invite members of the minority community and minority organizations to serve on permanent and ad hoc committees or commissions of the college. In that way, community colleges establish a direct network with the minority community, which they can exploit when positions open. Arrangements are made by some community colleges with local minority businesses to give release time to employees to teach on a part-time basis as visiting professors. One of the few positive aspects of the current slow economic climate is that many professionals are considering teaching as a new career, either on a temporary or permanent basis. Some companies even offer training for their employees interested in making the transition to the classroom.

Conclusion

Americans are temperamental and philosophical voyagers, alternately idealistic and practical. What began as a benevolent impulse to invite those from underprivileged communities to participate fully in the opportunities available to the larger society has been transformed to an agenda motivated by, among other things, enlightened self-interest. A subtle shift has occurred in the emphasis given to the benefits of higher education. No longer is educational attainment exclusively, or even primarily, a personal possession—something of value to the individual only. An educated populace—especially an educated minority population—is now seen as a community property, essential to the economic and social well-being of the society at large. Education certainly improves the life prospects of the individual, but more than ever before, education is featured as critical for the future of the community and nation. The ability of the nation's workers (especially its minority workers) to acquire higher skills will determine not only whether individual workers will be able to fill higher skilled jobs, but whether the nation will have those higher skilled jobs at all.

References

Access Is Not Enough: Report to the President Concerning Opportunities for Blacks at the University of Maryland at College Park. College Park: University of Maryland at College Park, 1989.

Education Commission of the States and the State Higher Education Executive Officers. *Focus on Minorities: Trends in Higher Education Participation and Success.* Denver, Colo.: Education Commission of the States and the State Higher Education Executive Officers, 1987.

Educational Testing Service. *ETS Policy Notes,* 1992, 5 (2), 12.

Magner, D. K. "Duke U. Struggles to Make Good on Pledge to Hire Black Professors." *Chronicle of Higher Education,* Mar. 1993, pp. A13–A15.

Richardson, R. C. *Institutional Climate and Minority Achievement.* Denver, Colo.: Education Commission of the States, 1989.

Richardson, R. C., Matthews, D. A., and Finney, J. E. *Improving State and Campus Environments for Quality and Diversity: A Self-Assessment.* Denver, Colo.: Education Commission of the States, 1992.

Workforce 2000, Executive Summary. Paper prepared for the White House Conference on Library and Information Services, July 9–13, 1991. (ED 337 193)

PIEDAD F. ROBERTSON *is secretary of education, Commonwealth of Massachusetts.*

TED FRIER *is special assistant to the secretary of education, Commonwealth of Massachusetts.*

A dramatic change in the demographics of Phoenix public schools led the Maricopa Community College System to take forceful steps to diversify its faculty and staff.

Minority Faculty Recruitment and Retention Strategies: The Maricopa Experience

Alfredo G. de los Santos, Jr.

Recent studies have shown clearly that the demographics of the students in America's schools have changed—students enrolled today represent a rich and diverse racial, ethnic, and cultural heritage. These studies further report the impact of this diversity on the country's institutions of higher education. No segment of higher education has reflected the demographic change more than the nation's community colleges. The community colleges enroll a very large proportion of the racial/ethnic minorities who enroll in institutions of higher education. In their tenth annual report issued in January 1992, the American Council on Education reported that "African American and Hispanics relied heavily on the nation's two-year colleges. In 1988, 47 percent of Hispanic first-time freshman attended two-year schools" (American Council on Education, 1992, p. 7).

In its 1993 report, the Commission to Improve Minority Education of the American Association of Community Colleges indicated that "Among ethnic minority undergraduate students, community colleges enroll 57 percent of American Indians, 59 percent of Hispanics, 45 percent of African Americans, and 44 percent of Asian/Pacific Islanders" (p. 7).

Despite the presence of minority students on community college campuses, racial/ethnic minorities are underrepresented among the full-time faculty in two-year colleges. In a 1992 "Research Briefs" issued by the American Council on Education, Carter and Ottinger reported that 93 percent of all male full-time faculty in community colleges and 89 percent of all female full-time faculty were white. African Americans represent only three percent of all male full-time faculty and six percent of female full-time faculty; American Indians represent two percent of male faculty and one percent of female faculty. Asian Americans constitute two percent of the males and two percent of the females. Hispanics represent two percent of each gender (Carter and Ottinger, 1992, p. 4).

Student Demographics in Phoenix Public Schools, 1986–87

The demographic changes in higher education are also reflected in the public schools, as racial/ethnic minorities now comprise the majority of students enrolled in most of the nation's largest cities. In Phoenix, Arizona, this reversal from minority to majority status at the high school level occurred in the late 1980s. During the 1987–88 academic year, then-superintendent of the Phoenix Union School District, Tim Dyer, made a series of presentations to community groups, civic organizations, and governmental agencies describing the student body enrolled in the ten-high-school system. Dyer explained that for the first time in the history of the school district, during the 1986–87 school year, the majority of the students were minority students. In 1967, only 20 percent of the students in the school district were minorities. Ten years later, the proportion of minority students had increased to 33 percent. By 1988, minorities comprised more than 52 percent of the total enrollment.

Superintendent Dyer outlined many of the factors that affect student retention and achievement in schools, particularly in urban settings. Among these are poverty, high unemployment, teen-aged pregnancy, lack of transportation, gangs, and poor housing. He made it clear that these factors, and not race and ethnicity, are closely related to retention and achievement.

Implications for the Maricopa Community Colleges

Superintendent Dyer's presentation to the governing board of the Maricopa Community Colleges during the Fall 1987 semester led to four general statements. The first was that unless the civic, political, and educational leadership worked to solve the social problems, the number of students graduating from the system would decrease and a smaller pool of graduates would be available to enroll in institutions of higher education, including the community colleges.

The second was that the racial/ethnic mix of the students who did graduate from the Phoenix Union School District would be very different from that of previous years. Thus, the graduates who would subsequently enroll in the community colleges would be much more diverse and the majority would before long be racial/ethnic minorities.

Third, because of this diversity, the students who would enroll in the community colleges would bring with them languages, values, cultures, and views quite different from previous student bodies. And finally, if and when the students who dropped out from the high schools did enroll in one of the community colleges, they would need educational, student, social, and cultural services that the institutions were not prepared to provide. Thus, the implications for the Maricopa Community Colleges were clear.

Maricopa Community Colleges

The Maricopa County Community College District (MCCCD), founded in 1962, consists of ten community colleges and centers, plus the Maricopa Skills Center. Each fall more than 90,000 students enroll in credit courses. The estimated year-round unduplicated enrollment for the 1991–92 academic year is 170,000. It is the nation's second-largest multi-college district, exceeded only by the Los Angeles system. The Maricopa system is the largest single provider of higher education in Arizona.

Governing Board Imperative

The governing board of the Maricopa Community Colleges which had supported efforts to increase the diversity of students, faculty and administrative staff since the late 1970s–early 1980s, began to take more active, forceful steps in 1987–88 to help the community colleges prepare for the change these students would bring with them.

The governing board created a Student Demographics Task Force, chaired by one of the board members, to review in more detail the demographic data and make recommendations. As a result a number of bridge programs were begun at the colleges. Subsequently the name of the task force was changed to the "At-Risk Student Task Force"; more recently the name was changed again, to the "Student Success Task Force." It continues to provide leadership and support.

In addition, the governing board created an Affirmative Action Task Force in 1988, also chaired by one of the board members. This task force helped develop strategies for the recruitment and retention of faculty and staff and monitored progress in the hiring process.

The governing board, at the March 1991 meeting, received the final report of the task force and approved, in principle, the seven major recommendations. The governing board referred the report to the vice-chancellor for human resources with instructions to implement where feasible, study when necessary, and modify when required. A semi-annual report regarding the implementation of the task force's recommendation is made to the governing board.

Executive Leadership

The executive leadership—the chancellor, vice-chancellors, and presidents—have been committed to build a diverse employee work force. Paul A. Elsner, MCCCD's chancellor, has been forceful in the district's effort to hire minority faculty and administrators. In the early 1980s he tried a number of initiatives, including creating a pool of money beyond the normal annual budget for each college, to be used especially to hire minority faculty.

He also convened the departmental chairs—most of whom were white men at the time—and met alone with them. Because of their mid-management positions and their power as the persons who screen and recommend candidates, he thought it was important to meet with them. He discussed with them the changing demographics in the public schools and the need for the community colleges to diversify the faculty. In addition, he spoke frequently at the meetings with the college presidents and vice-chancellors and urged them to follow through.

Approaches Used

Over the years, Maricopa Community Colleges have tried different approaches to creating applicant pools for faculty positions that have minority and female candidates in proportion to their availability. Many of these approaches are similar to those used by other institutions of higher education, including advertising in such publications as *The Chronicle of Higher Education, Black Issues in Higher Education,* and *Academe.* Advertisements have been placed in other publications as well, including *Hispanic Hot Line* and *Cambio.*

In addition, many other approaches were used. For example, faculty and staff visited universities and colleges with large minority enrollments. Candidates were interviewed face to face, and information about each person was included in an applicant-tracking system.

During the 1989–90 academic year, the recruitment effort included direct mailings to department chairs at major universities that offered at least the master's degree in disciplines in which faculty were needed. In addition, advertisements were placed in newspapers in six major cities, announcing orientation sessions. Possible candidates were interviewed by faculty and staff in hotels in those cities.

During the 1990–91 academic year, other approaches were used, including direct mailing (250 pieces) to the math departments at institutions of higher education with large minority enrollment. Advertisements were placed in the student newspapers at California university campuses and in the local newspapers. Recruitment and application packets were mailed directly to minority individuals using the Minority Graduate Data Base.

The direct mail campaign proved to be both successful in achieving minority hires and cost effective on a cost-per-hire basis. During 1991–92, the direct mail campaign was expanded to include databases that focused on specific minority groups, women, and disabled individuals.

The involvement of minority faculty and state and district minority organizations in the recruitment and orientation efforts has been a critical, significant part of the strategies used by the Maricopa Community Colleges. The minority leadership has been involved not only in the development of recruitment plans, but also in the implementation—from recruitment to participation in selection committees. Every year assessment was made of each approach used, including the number of candidates yielded and the number of actual hires made from these pools. If one initiative was not productive, others were then tried.

Results of Efforts

The results of these efforts are shown in Table 8.1. The number of minority full-time faculty members employed at the Maricopa Community Colleges increased from 127 in 1987, when they represented 16.2 percent of the total, to 176 in 1992 or 19.2 percent of the total faculty population of 913.

The absolute number of full-time faculty for all four of the racial/ethnic groups increased from the years 1987 to 1991; the proportion of the total faculty that they represented also increased. The number of African American full-time faculty increased from 41 in 1987 to 52 in 1992. Hispanic full-time faculty increased from 62 in 1987 to 89 in 1992, and ten additional Asian/Pacific Islander full-time faculty were employed, increasing their numbers from 14 to 24. Three additional American Indian full-time faculty were hired, raising the total from 10 to 13.

It should be noted that the numbers represent the district totals; the representation of racial/ethnic minorities on the faculty at each of the ten colleges in the Maricopa system is different. This is also true across the departments. The faculty at some colleges and in some departments do reflect ethnic diversity, but not every department at every college has achieved racial/ethnic diversity.

Institutional Climate

In order for affirmative action programs to succeed, building a faculty that represents the racial/ethnic mix of the student body and the community and

Table 8.1. Racial/Ethnic Characteristics of Full-Time Faculty, 1987 and 1992

Group	1987		1992	
	Number	Percentage	Number	Percentage
African American	41	5.2%	50	5.5%
Hispanic	62	7.9	89	9.7
Asian/Pacific Islander	14	1.8	24	2.6
Native American	10	1.3	13	1.4
Total minority	127	16.2	176	19.2
Total positions	787		913	

retaining a diverse faculty, a positive institutional climate must exist. Without the leadership of the governing board and the executive leadership, it is difficult, if not impossible to create such a climate. The building and maintenance of a positive institutional climate requires persistence and adequate resources.

Governing board. An institutional climate conducive to diversity of the faculty at the Maricopa Community Colleges has been created by the interest and commitment of the members of the governing board. The results of this are also reflected in the racial/ethnic mix of the executive leadership and management team.

For example, of the ten presidents, three are female. One of the four vice-chancellors is Hispanic. The racial/ethnic mix of the management groups, both in 1987 and in 1992, is shown in Table 8.2. The management team included a variety of positions, from deans to directors, technical staff, and coordinators, all nonfaculty. The total number of minority managers increased from 66 in 1987, when they represented 19.6 percent of the total, to 91 in 1992, when they represented 23.2 percent. The number of African American managers increased from 20 in 1987 to 26 in 1992, while the number of Hispanic managers increased from 34 to 53 during the same time period. The number of Asians or Pacific Islanders decreased from five to four; the number of Native American managers increased from seven to eight.

Executive group. The leadership of the executive group is crucial to the climate of the institution. The executive group must not only define the policies that lead to diversity, but must communicate these policies to the total institutions—repeatedly, often, forcefully. And finally, the executive group must "walk the talk"; that is, they must demonstrate through example of a commitment to diversity. The Maricopa executive group has encouraged and supported the development of a number of minority employee organizations. The leadership of these various groups meet regularly with the executive administration to discuss issues and suggest solutions to various problems facing minority employees and the district itself. The feedback and input from these groups has strengthened the awareness of the executive leadership with respect to minority issues.

Table 8.2. Racial/Ethnic Characteristics of Management Group, 1987 and 1992

| Group | 1987 | | 1992 | |
	Number	Percentage	Number	Percentage
African American	20	5.9%	26	6.6%
Hispanic	34	10.1	53	13.4
Asian/Pacific Islander	5	1.5	4	1.0
Native American	7	2.1	8	2.0
Total minority	66	19.6	91	23.2
Total positions	338		392	

Persistence. The implementation of policies leading to diversity of the faculty and staff requires persistence at every level of the institution. D. V. Gares and E. A. Delco, Jr., outlined ten "action steps" in order for a community college district to have success in the recruitment, hiring, and retention of minorities from support of the board of trustees, presidents, and academic administration to faculty support, recruiting, screening, interviewing, selection, and orientation and support (Gares and Delco, 1991, pp. 103–108).

For these ten "action steps" to succeed, the department chairs, the members of the minority groups and organizations, the members of the screening committees, the deans, the staff in the human resources and employment office, and others . . . all must be persistent in their effort. All must persevere because building a diverse faculty is hard work.

Resources. Needless to say, appropriate resources must be provided for the effort to succeed, both human and fiscal. The office that coordinates the recruitment and hiring processes must have enough staff—qualified, competent, committed—to support the recruitment, screening, and hiring of candidates. This staff should provide orientation and training to the faculty and staff who serve on the screening committees so that they can understand the district's commitment and the laws, rules, and regulations that pertain.

Adequate fiscal resources must be made available to carry out comprehensive, effective hiring processes—from advertising in national, regional, and local media to sending faculty and staff (particularly racial/ethnic minorities) to participate in recruitment trips when appropriate.

Conclusion

The dramatic change in the demographics in the public schools in Phoenix, Arizona, has important implications for the Maricopa County Community College District. The students who will graduate from the schools and subsequently enroll in the community colleges will be very different from their predecessors; they will be much more diverse and will bring with them a variety of languages, values, ideals, and cultures. In order to serve the needs of these students, the governing board and the executive leadership took forceful steps to diversify faculty and staff. A variety of approaches were used over a five-year period. The success of these efforts is reflected in the current composition of the faculty and staff. Such efforts require the involvement and commitment of the governing board and the executive leadership along with sufficient resources to ensure success.

References

American Association of Community Colleges, Commission to Improve Minority Education. *Making Good on Our Promises ... Moving Beyond Rhetoric to Action.* Washington, D.C.: American Association of Community Colleges, 1993.

American Council on Education. *Minorities in Higher Education.* Tenth Annual Status Report 1991. Washington, D.C.: American Council on Education, 1992.

Carter, D. J., and Ottinger, C. A. "Community College Faculty: A Profile." *Research Briefs,* 1992, 3 (7).

Gares, D. V., and Delco, E. A., Jr. "Ten Steps in Successful Minority Hiring and Retention." In D. Angel and A. Barrera (eds.), *Rethinking Minority Enrollment.* New Directions for Community Colleges, no. 74. San Francisco: Jossey-Bass, 1991.

ALFREDO G. DE LOS SANTOS, JR., is vice-chancellor for educational development at Maricopa Community College in Tempe, Arizona.

New groups bring varying cultural perspectives to an institution and must undergo a period of negotiating differences with the established forces of the community college.

Critical Perspectives on Community College Education

James Valadez

The culture of an educational institution is reflected in the values, traditions, rituals, and the system of beliefs of the faculty, staff, and students. The culture of an institution is often deeply embedded and changes come slowly. Institutional culture is also a major influence in shaping the policies and practices of the organization (Schein, 1992). These policies and practices are products of the "taken for granted attitudes" of the members of the organization. Decisions are made and frequently swayed by these attitudes simply because they represent ways of doing things that have been routine for years. Organizations often have standard-bearers or those designated to maintain the culture of the institution (Schein, 1992). These are usually people with knowledge of the history and practices of the institution who are in positions of power or influence. Through this system, those with cultural knowledge are able to transmit information and socialize newcomers into the organization. The ability of newcomers to learn and adapt to the culture of the organization has a significant impact on the level of success they will have in this new setting.

Because culture is a socially constructed process in which new members of a society learn the traditions, values, and nuances of the social system, learning the culture involves acquiring the information from more knowledgeable members of the society. The process may not be entirely one-sided, however. Learning the culture of an organization involves negotiation between members of the society regarding the meaning of cultural practices. Newcomers may come into an organization with their own ideas about how to accomplish tasks, and these methods may not be in congruence with the practices of the organization. The negotiation of meaning can result in conflict that leads to either resolution or struggle.

This study examines the institutional culture of a small rural institution in the southeastern United States. To examine the culture, I took a critical perspective to account for the interplay of race, class, and culture with the institutional arrangements and practices of the institution. I examined the tension between the established traditional practices of the college and the meanings associated with those practices by the faculty, staff, and students of the institution. The purpose of examining the culture of the institution was to reflect on how cultural practices (including the values and traditional methods of decision making) influenced institutional policies.

Critical Ethnography

Critical ethnography is a form of empirical research in which the researcher attempts to represent a culture, consciousness, or the lived experiences of oppressed people living in asymmetrical power relations (Quantz, 1992). Critical ethnographers do not merely describe oppressed groups, but examine why these groups are marginalized, how they participate in society, and how the researcher's understanding of oppressed groups could contribute to the restructuring of their positions. This orienting framework motivates the researcher to conduct the study, helps to formulate the questions, and influences the selection of the problem to be studied and the sites to be selected (Carspecken and Apple, 1992). The subject of the research is formed in an exchange with the participants throughout the research process. The topic for the present study was selected because of the importance of community college education to minorities, women, and working-class students. Community colleges are the institution of choice for these groups, and a thorough analysis of race, class, and culture within the institution is needed to reach an understanding of the community college culture. This research would have implications not only for the retention of minority students, but for the long-range development and encouragement of these groups to pursue all forms of postsecondary education. Since community colleges represent the point of entry for so many minority students, it is hoped that the community college will provide a future starting point for the development of minority faculty.

Data Collection and Analysis

The study centered on describing the processes that contributed to the development and maintenance of an institutional culture. I collected the data through ethnographic interviews, examination of institutional documents, and observations over a period of fourteen months. I conducted over a hundred interviews with faculty, staff, students, and administrators. I selected participants using maximum variation sampling (Patton, 1990). This strategy allowed me to select participants with widely different experiences and varying backgrounds. The purpose in using this method was to describe variation within a group and to search for common or disparate themes in the data.

The interviews addressed several core areas: faculty, staff, and student beliefs and values about education and their perceptions of the institution's willingness to change to accommodate the needs of a changing population. In addition to the formal interviews, numerous informal interviews with the president and vice-president of the college occurred. The purpose of these informal interviews was to share data and to get an insider's perspective on the findings (Agar, 1980; Bogdan and Biklen, 1992). These ongoing conversations were useful in confirming some of the researchers ideas and in revealing new perspectives on the data.

The analytic strategy used was based on the constant comparative method described by Glaser and Strauss (1967). With this strategy categories are formed and revised as the data are being collected. This strategy is compatible with a critical perspective in which the researcher follows a dialectical process in order to theorize about the social problems of everyday life with an eye toward solving them (Fay, 1977).

Setting

The setting for this case study was Eastlake Community College (fictitious name) in eastern North Carolina. Eastlake is located in a small rural county in a largely rural state. The population of the county is approximately 76,000 with whites comprising 68 percent of the population and African Americans 31 percent (Bureau of the Census, 1990). A small but growing Latino population, the majority of whom are agricultural workers, resides in the county. There is wide disparity of income in the county, with a large number of African Americans either unemployed or employed in low-skill and low-paying service or manufacturing jobs. The median family income for whites in the county is $31,000, compared with the median family income of $19,000 for African Americans (State Data Center, 1991).

Traditionalists

A conflict existed at the community college between two groups of people whom I will label traditionalists and iconoclasts. Traditionalists in the institution were generally those faculty and staff who had been at the institution for a number of years and assumed a role that Schein (1992) described as the "standard bearers of the organization." These were individuals who knew how "it had always been done" at the institution and also had a sense for the history and traditions of the institution. Traditionalists attempted to maintain the standards of the institution by enforcing policies that had historical significance to the institution, and also represented time-honored procedures such as methods for teaching and evaluating students. These faculty and staff had expectations that students should conform to their perceptions of appropriate college student behavior. A faculty member I interviewed said this about her instructional approaches: "We would like to get the students to speak properly, dress well. We tell them we are preparing them for the world of work. Some students don't have any idea what we're talking about. It's all totally new to them, and we're trying to fill in for a lot information they should already have."

The comments by the faculty member reflect a belief that students must adapt their behavior to existing standards or norms. If students do not master these standards, they may be judged negatively. When asked if she thought other faculty felt the same way about maintaining standards, this faculty member stated: "I understand that there are other faculty who do not penalize for late work. I personally feel that we are not doing the students any favors when we let get away with substandard work. We can't spoon feed them forever."

In general, the traditionalist faculty were well-meaning and were concerned about the success of students. There was never any question in their minds whether they were treating all students fairly and equitably. They expressed opinions such as the following: "This institution provides the opportunity for any student to make it. Any student who wants to work hard can accomplish anything she wants to here. If a student wants to go into nursing there's no reason why he or she can't study hard and make it."

A predominant attitude among traditionalists was that the institution provided the opportunity, and it was up to the individual to make the most of it. Traditionalists did not consider that the practices of the institution might present barriers to some students but viewed the situation as a process by which qualified and hard-working students could rise to the top. The attitude of traditionalists is that the educational institution is a neutral site in which all individuals are judged fairly. If individuals do not do well or drop out, traditionalists are more likely to place the blame on the students and absolve their institution of any fault.

The attitude that the institution is a neutral site therefore minimizes the need for adapting it to meet the cultural needs of a diverse student body. This attitude also lessens the need for the institution to make efforts to look within the institution to examine policies or procedures that are creating barriers for minority student academic achievement. This lack of perspective may also contribute to the creation of an institutional climate that fails to recognize the strengths and contributions of minority groups, and as a result may be perceived as hostile to minority students, faculty, and staff.

Iconoclasts

The iconoclasts of the institution were those faculty and staff who believed that the institution had to make adjustments to fulfill the broader needs of the community. The community served by the community college was populated by a high proportion of African Americans (31 percent), yet only 20 percent of the college enrollment was African American. White students dominated some disciplines, particularly those in the allied health sciences. In comparison, African American students were overrepresented in the developmental studies area. Many of the African American students have aspirations to enroll in the college transfer majors or the allied health programs but found that placement tests, curricular demands, or other requirements acted as barriers in their path. Faculty and administrators were aware of these problems, but solutions have been elusive.

Iconoclasts have definite ideas for instituting change, but their ideas have met with resistance. When interviewed, a faculty member had this to say about the problem: "There is a real testing mentality here. Those placement tests mean everything. I know that some students are scared to death of those tests. They can't pass the tests, so they can't get into the nursing program."

Because few minorities ever get into these programs, chances diminish for developing students who will enter the professions and eventually become faculty members in nursing, physical therapy, or other programs dominated by white students and faculty. The need for minority faculty was frequently cited by the iconoclasts of the institution. An administrator who was interviewed commented about an African American faculty member: "Miranda makes such a difference. She can talk to the [African American] students. She knows how to communicate, she calls them, she finds out what the problem is. I can see the difference."

Iconoclasts attempt to press the issue of change but continue to struggle with the traditionalists. A major point of contention centers around the method of evaluating students. The method of evaluation seems to reflect the philosophical values of the two groups. Traditionalists believe that the only fair way to evaluate students is through some standardized measure in which all students have an equal chance of success. In their belief, this unbiased measure gives all students who want to work hard an equal opportunity. The iconoclasts argue, however, that the measure is not inherently neutral and that other measures may be appropriate for evaluating students. The iconoclasts also recognize the need for diversifying the institution to provide broader perspectives, to provide more role models for minority students, and to strengthen the institution by including more groups into the system.

Discussion

The college in this study was the site of conflict between the established forces of education and the newly emerging groups who are establishing their presence in the community colleges. The new groups bring cultural attributes to the college, and their beliefs and values sometimes conflict with those of the established group. The established group of faculty and administrators, the traditionalists in the institution, form the majority and promote the idea that these newcomers need to adapt to existing structures.

Faculty, staff, and administrators at Eastlake, because of their own social and educational backgrounds, have certain expectations and values associated with education. The "standard-bearers" or traditionalists expect that newcomers will conform or will attain what they believe to be the norms or standards of the established group—including dress, language, and values.

Most faculty members attempted to make adjustments for the students, but many of the "taken-for-granted" institutional arrangements and practices such as styles of teaching and assessment remained in force.

A critical perspective calls for community college administrators and faculty to examine current practices and institutional arrangements that may have historical and traditional significance to the institution but do not contribute to opening the institution to values, traditions, and beliefs of minority groups. Administrators, faculty, and staff must understand that the traditional values and culture of higher education do not reflect the culture and traditions of minority groups. Movement toward opening the institution to these new perspectives would reaffirm the community college's commitment toward providing equal opportunity for all people.

References

Agar, M. H. *The Professional Stranger*. New York: Academic Press, 1980.

Bogdan, R., and Biklen, S. *Qualitative Research for Education: An Introduction to Theory and Methods*. Needham Heights, Mass.: Allyn & Bacon, 1992.

Bureau of the Census. *1990 Census of the Population*. Washington, D.C.: U.S. Government Printing Office, 1990.

Carspecken, P. F., and Apple, M. "Critical Qualitative Research: Theory, Methodology and Practice." In M. D. LeCompte, W. L. Millroy, and J. Preissle (eds.), *The Handbook of Qualitative Research in Education*. San Diego: Academic Press, 1992.

Fay, B. *Social Theory and Political Practice*. London: George Allen and Unwin, 1977.

Glaser, B. G., and Strauss, A. L. *The Discovery of Grounded Theory*. Chicago: Aldine, 1967.

Patton, M. Q. *Qualitative Evaluation and Research Methods*. Newbury Park, Calif.: Sage, 1990.

Quantz, R. A. "On Critical Ethnography (With Some Postmodern Considerations)." In M. D. LeCompte, W. L. Millroy, and J. Preissle (eds.), *The Handbook of Qualitative Research in Education*. San Diego: Academic Press, 1992.

Schein, E. H. *Organizational Culture and Leadership*. (2nd ed.) San Francisco: Jossey-Bass, 1992.

State Data Center. *Statistical Abstract of North Carolina Counties*. Raleigh, N.C.: Office of State Budget and Management, 1991.

JAMES VALADEZ is assistant professor of adult and community college education at North Carolina State University in Raleigh.

An annotated bibliography is provided that reflects major issues involved in the recruitment and retention of community college minority faculty, including abstracts of articles on state-level diversity plans, on developing a pipeline for minority faculty to teach at two-year colleges, and on the role of leadership and its ability to affect community college diversity.

Sources and Information: Recruiting and Maintaining Minority Faculty

Frankie S. Laanan

Almost half the minority students in higher education are in community colleges but they are not met by a proportional representation of minority faculty. Many of these colleges have taken active measures to recruit and retain a diverse population of employees, but the still-sparse representation of minority faculty in general, and minority women faculty in particular, is a continuing challenge.

The following publications reflect the current ERIC literature on recruiting and maintaining community college minority faculty. They also represent the efforts to create environments that promote cultural diversity in the workforce. Most ERIC documents (publications with ED numbers) can be viewed on microfiche at over nine hundred libraries worldwide. In addition, most may be ordered on microfiche or on paper from the ERIC Document Reproduction Service (EDRS) by calling (800) 443-ERIC. Journal articles are not available from EDRS, but they can be acquired through regular library channels or purchased from the University Microfilm International Articles Clearinghouse at (800) 521–0600, extension 533.

General Articles

These articles provide an overview of issues regarding the underrepresentation of women and ethnic minority faculty in American two-year colleges.

Calathes, William. "Perpetuating Social Inequalities." *Thought and Action*, 1990, 7 (2), 137–154.

A review of the literature on minority underrepresentation in higher education and issues specific to community colleges suggests several solutions, including improved institutional commitment to hiring for diversity among faculty and administrators, multicultural expertise as a qualification for some positions, more hospitable campus and classroom environments, and better student services.

Gillett-Karam, R., Roueche, S. D., and Roueche, J. E. "Underrepresentation and the Question of Diversity." *Community, Technical, and Junior College Journal,* 1991, *61* (3), 22–25.

Emphasizes the leadership role of community college faculty in developing critical teaching strategies to focus attention on the needs of women and minorities. This article describes six facets of teaching excellence: engaging students' desire to learn, increasing opportunities, eliminating obstacles, empowering students through high expectations, offering positive guidance, and motivating students toward independence.

Jones, B. B. "Working with the 'Only One' in the Division." Paper presented at the 2nd Annual International Conference for Community College Chairs, Deans, and Other Instructional Leaders, Phoenix, February 17–20, 1993. 13 pp. (ED 354 935)

This paper examines the experiences of minority faculty members and administrators who may be the "only one"—the token minority—within their division by combining a review of the literature with interviews. Five African Americans, two Hispanics, one Native American, one Asian, one female, and two physically handicapped vocational education instructors were interviewed. Interview respondents shared common perceptions and experiences, including the following: (1) the tendency of other people to enlarge or generalize the respondents' comments or behaviors to the groups that they represent, often leading to overachieving behavior; (2) social and professional isolation, often leading to feelings of loneliness; (3) encounters with false assumptions and stereotypes, including prejudice and lack of professional respect or advancement from peers; (4) expectations to serve on multiple committees within their division to represent a minority perspective, and also to serve as community leaders for their particular minority group; and (5) difficulties in dealing with accepted, if unrecognized, norms of white and male privilege, the tyranny of the majority, racism, and biases. Those interviewed cited professional acknowledgement and respect, acknowledgement of individual uniqueness, recognition and utilization of expertise, professional trust, honest evaluations, and inclusion in collegial networks as elements of the preferred professional environment.

Hahn, T. C. *Future Faculty Development Program.* Chula Vista, Calif.: Southwestern College, 1990. 12 pp. (ED 325 156)

Hahn discusses the program developed by Southwestern College (SC) called the Future Faculty Development Program. The purpose of the program is to develop a pool of qualified candidates for full-time faculty positions to reflect the adult population of California. The program purpose is fourfold: (1) to provide a unique opportunity for current students and recent alumni of SC to develop those talents, skills, and qualifications necessary to prepare for a career in community college teaching or counseling; (2) to provide the opportunity for such individuals to become employed by the district in one of three differentiated staffing levels (Work Study or Federal Work Study, Internships, and Instructional Assistantships) under the mentorship of supervising faculty and staff; (3) to provide the means for a proactive institutional response to the affirmative action mandates of Assembly Bill 1725 and the near future prospect of massive faculty and staff retirements; and (4) to assist the college district in meeting the goal of reflecting the ethnic composition of the college's service territory by providing sufficient numbers of minority role models in staffing positions.

Diversity Plans at State Levels

Several states have established effective plans to address the issues of minority faculty recruitment to meet the future needs of their diverse student populations.

Texas Higher Education Coordinating Board. *A Study of Faculty Needs in Texas, 1991–2008. A Report to the Texas Higher Education Coordinating Board by the Faculty Shortages Advisory Committee.* Austin: Texas Higher Education Coordinating Board, 1992. 110 pp. (ED 359 869)
   This report predicts that, during the next two decades, Texas colleges and universities will have increasing enrollments with larger increases in minority students. Quantitative and anecdotal evidence indicates faculty hiring will become more difficult in this and the next decade if current trends continue, particularly in minority faculty where there already exists a shortage of African American and Hispanic college faculty. This report examines the faculty shortage needs of Texas in the public senior universities and junior colleges and makes a determination of how the state will be affected by the projected nationwide shortages. The report recommends approaches to alleviating the expected problems which focus on increased efficiency in the use of faculty resources, increased production of doctoral degree holders, and efforts to increase the number of minority graduate students.

Wolfe, G. F. "Recruiting Minorities into Teaching: A Joint Registration Model." *Community College Journal*, 1993, 63 (4), 32–35.
   This article discusses the shortage of African American teachers to serve as educational role models and describes New York State's program allowing

minority students to enter teacher education programs jointly at two- and four-year institutions. Wolfe reviews advantages of joint enrollment efforts and program characteristics of top proposals submitted to the State Department of Education.

Deese, S., and McKay, S. *The Dawning of a New Century: North Carolina Community College System. Comprehensive Plan for Administrative Leadership Through Diversity Enhancement. A Report to the System President.* Raleigh: North Carolina Community College System, 1991. 52 pp. (ED 341 437)

This report from the North Carolina Community College System (NCCCS) presents a series of recommendations for the promotion and recruitment of minorities and women for the senior-level administrative staff of the NCCCS. The report includes information on past efforts to recruit and promote women and minorities on the staff of the NCCCS as well as at individual community colleges; provides current data on the ethnic and gender composition of the student body, faculty, and administration of North Carolina's community colleges; and reviews hiring trends nationwide and in the NCCCS. The report presents twenty-six recommendations on issues relating to the role of leadership, increased funding, regional seminars, effective applicant pool strategies, and creation of an oversight committee.

Ballobin, K., Rush, P., and Wisialowski, J. "A Cultural Diversity Plan." Paper presented at the 98th annual meeting of the North Central Association of Colleges and Schools, Chicago, April 4–6, 1993. 9 pp. (ED 356 021)

This paper discusses Platte Campus of Central Community College in Columbus, Nebraska, and its efforts in working with nine other colleges to promote cultural and work force diversity at the colleges. The goals of the project were to expand programs to accommodate leadership diversity, design innovative staff development programs, develop personnel practices to enhance the recruitment and retention of women and minorities, provide in-service training in using curriculum components and classroom techniques that foster multicultural sensitivity, and disseminate information about project activities. The Platte Cultural Diversity Task Force Committee was formed to encourage campus-wide participation and support, educate campus leaders, and coordinate activities with other campuses. The Task Force plans encourage the development of different teaching styles, educate the campus community about diversity issues, and promote a proactive role in the recruitment and retention of a diverse population of employees and students.

Pipeline for Minority Teachers

Given that close to 50 percent of minorities in college are enrolled in two-year institutions, this segment of higher education plays an integral role in serving as a delivery system of future minority teachers. Collaborative efforts between two-year colleges and baccalaureate-granting institutions may serve to increase the numbers of minority students entering teacher preparation at four-year institutions.

Anderson, B. J. "Community Colleges: Promises or Preclusions." Paper presented at the 17th annual convention of the American Mathematical Association of Two-Year Colleges, Seattle, November 7–10, 1991. 24 pp. (ED 351 045)
    This paper discusses how two-year institutions can play a critical role in serving as an educational pipeline in the mathematics discipline. Anderson asserts that nearly 10 percent of the students in the United States who receive doctorates in the mathematical sciences begin their studies at two-year institutions and that approximately 50 percent of minorities in college are enrolled in these institutions. Given this phenomenon, the role of these colleges in increasing minority participation in mathematics-related fields cannot be overstated. The paper presents ten proven strategies that can be implemented by other institutions as possible recommendations.

Anglin, L. W., and others. "The Missing Rung of the Teacher Education Ladder: Community Colleges." Paper presented at the 42nd annual meeting of the American Association of Colleges for Teacher Education, Atlanta, Feb. 27–Mar. 2, 1991. 16 pp. (ED 336 383)
    This paper discusses the rapid decline of the minority teaching population at two-year institutions. By reviewing previous barriers to community college student transfer into teacher education programs and recent trends creating a favorable atmosphere for such transfer, a case is built for incorporating community colleges as an important rung in the teacher-education ladder. A working model (The Teaching Leadership Consortium) for a community college-university minority teacher recruitment project is described. Recognizing that such recruitment efforts are complex and are further complicated by institutional barriers, the paper offers six recommendations for those considering the adoption of a similar recruitment strategy. These recommendations include a formal signed partnership agreement, a boundary spanner role, careful joint planning, coordinated student support systems, a community college pre-education curriculum, and field experience and preservice arrangements with local schools. Fourteen references are included.

Gutknecht, B., and others. "Preparation of Minority Educators (PREMIER): A Public School/Community College/University Collaborative Program." Paper presented at the 72nd annual meeting of the Association of Teacher Educators, Orlando, Fla., Feb. 15–19, 1992. 27 pp. (ED 346 049)
    This paper introduces PREMIER (Preparation of Minority Educators Partnership Program), designed to find ways to attract and retain more minority teachers in Florida schools. It is a collaborative effort among an urban school district (Duval County Public Schools), a local community college (Florida

Community College at Jacksonville), and an urban college of education (University of North Florida). PREMIER has five major goals: (1) to enhance cooperative links among the community college, the university, and the public schools in order to increase the number of minority students entering teacher preparation, improve students' chances of graduating from college, and facilitate the matriculation process from school to community college to university; (2) to identify and recruit more minority students from high schools and community colleges and provide mentoring experiences designed to support them through their undergraduate program; (3) to provide PREMIER students with academic support in basic skills needed for success in the teacher preparation program and in teaching; (4) to provide a wide range of early field experiences; and (5) to provide a counseling/mentoring support system to improve retention and program completion rates.

The Role of Leadership

Leadership plays a critical role in planning, developing, and implementing strategies to enhance diversity on the campuses.

Gillett-Karam, R., Roueche, S. D., and Roueche, J. E. *Underrepresentation and the Question of Diversity: Women and Minorities in the Community College.* Washington, D.C.: American Association of Community and Junior Colleges, 1991. 271 pp. (ED 331 551)

Within the context of the history of educational administration and related social movements in the United States, this book examines the underrepresentation of women and of racial and ethnic minorities in community college leadership. Chapter One, "Finding Equality in Egalitarian Educational Institutions," presents the premise of the book, that community colleges have not met their responsibilities to these underrepresented groups. In Chapter Two, "Confronting the Language of Diversity," the debates concerning equality and inequality, the meaning of justice, the critical role of culture, and American democracy and pluralism are explored. Chapter Three, "Women: Expression and Experience in Academic Literature," looks at the historical and philosophical premises upon which the "woman question" rests, and reviews recent findings concerning the role of women in education and leadership. In Chapter Four, "Minorities: Expression and Experience in Academic Literature," the dilemmas and controversies surrounding racial and ethnic equality are scrutinized, drawing on the legal and educational histories of minority groups. Chapter Five, "Affirmative Action: Then and Now," examines the issues and politics of social movements and their challenges to the status quo. In Chapter Six, "Inclusionary Practices: Highlighting Exemplary Programs," the achievements of several organizations, programs, and policies now existing throughout the United States are discussed. Chapter Seven, "What the Leaders Are Saying: The Voices of Diversity," presents the views of community college leaders from underrepresented groups. Finally, Chapter Eight, "Getting There from

Where You Are: Increasing Representation and Recognition," provides a time-line and strategies for transforming community colleges.

Gilliland, J. R. "Diversifying Leadership in Community Colleges." In D. Angel and A. Barrera (eds.), *Rekindling Minority Enrollment.* New Directions for Community Colleges, no. 74. San Francisco: Jossey-Bass, 1991.

Gilliland presents practical and theoretical reasons to support work force diversity, ways that leadership diversity strengthens an organization, progress toward leadership diversification in higher education and the private sector, stages of the leadership diversity cycle, and leadership diversification efforts at Metropolitan Community College in Nebraska.

Kappner, A. S. "The Role of Leadership in Planning and Implementing Diversity." Paper presented at the 71st annual national convention of the American Association of Community and Junior Colleges, Kansas City, Mo., Apr. 13–16, 1991. 28 pp. (ED 333 910)

Kappner describes Borough of Manhattan Community College's (BMCC) demographic breakdown and its low percentage of minority faculty. As a result of a systemwide administrative retreat, an ad hoc committee of city university presidents formed and developed a statement on diversity. In response to this statement, BMCC undertook efforts to recruit more bilingual counselors; infuse diversity issues into the freshman orientation curriculum; increase community outreach efforts; expand the affirmative action committee; initiate special programs and workshops in cross-cultural understanding and inter-group dynamics for faculty and staff; implement a pre-freshman basic skills program; develop a mentoring program for black students; and create a special seminar to assist women and minority faculty in completing their doctoral dissertations.

Sanchez, A. A. "Diversity in Leadership, Diversity in the Classroom." *Community College Journal,* 1993, 63 (3), 31–33.

Sanchez perceives the key challenge facing community colleges in the 1990s to be the development of leadership that represents the diversity of the colleges' students and local constituents. He further considers the components of a plan for changing institutional values, climate, and learning environment.

FRANKIE S. LAANAN is research assistant at the Center for the Study of Community Colleges, University of California, Los Angeles.

INDEX

ORDERING INFORMATION

NEW DIRECTIONS FOR COMMUNITY COLLEGES is a series of paperback books that provides expert assistance to help community colleges meet the challenges of their distinctive and expanding educational mission. Books in the series are published quarterly in Spring, Summer, Fall, and Winter and are available for purchase by subscription and individually.

SUBSCRIPTIONS for 1994 cost $49.00 for individuals (a savings of 25 percent over single-copy prices) and $72.00 for institutions, agencies, and libraries. Please do not send institutional checks for personal subscriptions. Standing orders are accepted.

SINGLE COPIES cost $16.95 when payment accompanies order. (California, New Jersey, New York, and Washington, D.C., residents please include appropriate sales tax.) All orders will be charged postage and handling.

DISCOUNTS FOR QUANTITY ORDERS are available. Please write to the address below for information.

ALL ORDERS must include either the name of an individual or an official purchase order number. Please submit your order as follows:
   Subscriptions: specify series and year subscription is to begin
   Single copies: include individual title code (such as CC82)

MAIL ALL ORDERS TO:
   Jossey-Bass Publishers
   350 Sansome Street
   San Francisco, California 94104-1342

FOR SUBSCRIPTION SALES OUTSIDE OF THE UNITED STATES, contact any international subscription agency or Jossey-Bass directly.